民航空中交通管理系列丛书

空中交通管制员无线电陆空通话

主编 王万乐 赵 琦

清华大学出版社
北京交通大学出版社
·北京·

内 容 简 介

本书是民航院校空管专业学生学习掌握基础无线电陆空通话的教材,内容按照飞行阶段组织,包括基本运行程序、机场管制、进近管制、区域管制和紧急情况,附录提供了国内外常见航空公司代码、话呼及公司名称。对于各个知识点,参考国际民航组织及我国相关文件,列出了常用单词和词组及英汉双语对照的通话范例。每个知识点由"听录音"引入,符合陆空通话的应用场景。读者可扫本书二维码下载录音文件。本书除用于空管专业学生之外,也可作为在职管制员准备管制员英语等级考试之用。本书有配套的练习册。

本书封面贴有清华大学出版社防伪标签,无标签者不得销售。
版权所有,侵权必究。侵权举报电话:010-62782989 13501256678 13801310933

图书在版编目(CIP)数据

空中交通管制员无线电陆空通话:英文 / 王万乐,赵琦主编. —北京:北京交通大学出版社:清华大学出版社,2016.5(2021.1 重印)
 ISBN 978-7-5121-2718-0

Ⅰ. ①空… Ⅱ. ①王… ②赵… Ⅲ. ①空中交通管制-陆空协同通信-英语-口语-高等学校-教材 Ⅳ. ①H319.9

中国版本图书馆 CIP 数据核字(2016)第 090125 号

空中交通管制员无线电陆空通话
KONGZHONG JIAOTONG GUANZHIYUAN WUXIANDIAN LU-KONG TONGHUA

责任编辑:谭文芳 助理编辑:龙嫚嫚	
出版发行:清 华 大 学 出 版 社 邮编:100084 电话:010-62776969 http://www.tup.com.cn	
北京交通大学出版社 邮编:100044 电话:010-51686414 http://www.bjtup.com.cn	
印 刷 者:北京虎彩文化传播有限公司	
经　　销:全国新华书店	
开　　本:185 mm×260 mm 印张:5.75 字数:142 千字	
版　　次:2016 年 5 月第 1 版 2021 年 1 月第 6 次印刷	
书　　号:ISBN 978-7-5121-2718-0/H • 447	
印　　数:4 101~4 700 册 定价:19.00 元	

本书如有质量问题,请向北京交通大学出版社质监组反映。对您的意见和批评,我们表示欢迎和感谢。
投诉电话:010-51686043,51686008;传真:010-62225406;E-mail:press@bjtu.edu.cn。

M⁺BOOK 版图书使用说明

● **如何安装**

扫描二维码，根据手机或平板电脑系统类型选择相应的应用程序，单击下载，安装在手机或平板电脑上（建议在 Wi-Fi 环境中下载）。

● **如何使用**

打开应用程序，注册账号并登录后，点击页面上方"扫一扫"，即可扫码添加您需要的书。选择任意一本下载好的图书，进入阅读界面。点击"纸飞机"图标，可以查看图书简介。点击"悦读"，即可查看图书全文（或图书相关信息）。

● **如何下载资源**

点击"图书附件"下方各图标即可下载图书附带的音频、视频、动画、3D 模型等多媒体资源。不加密的附件可长按分享至 PC 或其他终端。

具体操作详情请参考应用程序内置的《使用手册》。

前　言

无线电陆空通话（以下简称陆空通话）是当前空中交通服务单位与航空器之间进行话音通信的方式。正确使用陆空通话用语进行信息沟通，对航空器的安全高效运行有着至关重要的作用。历史上由于陆空通话不规范导致航空不安全事件甚至飞行事故的案例不胜枚举，为此，国际民航组织（ICAO）提出一系列英语语言标准和建议，强调了相关通话英语的重要性，并且在《ICAO 语言能力要求实施手册》（Doc9835/AN453）中明确了英语语言熟练程度的评判标准。从事国际飞行的航空器驾驶员（以下简称驾驶员）和空中交通管制员（以下简称管制员）须达到相应英语通话标准要求，除了使用 ICAO 规定的标准术语（phraseology）以外，还必须能够用简明英语（plain language）准确、简洁、无误地进行交流。中国民用航空局空中交通管理局要求管制员必须达到 ICAO 所要求的管制员英语等级四级及以上水平。

陆空通话作为驾驶员和管制员在整个飞行过程中按照一定程序进行交流、沟通的语言，具有很强的专业性和情境性。陆空通话教学的根本目的就是提高学生实际应用英语通话的能力，主要是"听"与"说"方面，让学生具备在非面对面的情况下准确实现信息交流的能力。学生从开始接触陆空通话到正确、熟练地应用标准术语以至达到"脱口而出"的程度，需要一个长期的、科学的学习、练习和应用过程。本书针对民航院校空管专业学生，以陆空通话术语为核心，在内容编排上以飞行流程为主线，从"听"入手，形成对陆空通话应用情境的基本认识，再结合实例、示意图等讲述飞行各阶段的标准通话术语，旨在将通话内容的学习与练习置于空管运行情境中，使学生在具体的场景中练习通话、提高能力。此外，本书从 ICAO 语言熟练要求出发，即以发音、结构、词汇、流利程度、理解能力和互动 6 个方面为着眼点设计了大量的听说练习，充分体现"学练结合、以练代学、练中生技"的学习方法和规律，旨在培养学生基本的陆空通话能力和习惯，为将来进入空管岗位进行更高阶段的培训打下坚实的基础。万丈高楼平地起，对于民航院校空管专业的学生来说，掌握基本的陆空通话术语并建立良好的通话习惯是学习期间必须不断努力追求的目标。

本书由中国民航大学空中交通管理学院教师王万乐和黄贻刚提出最初的编写思路和核心理念，王万乐和赵琦主编，英语课程组教师李学明、赵德斌、马丽娟、刘博、赵璐和刘永欣参编，终成此稿。本书共分为 7 章。第 1 章、第 4 章及第 7 章主要由王万乐和黄贻刚编写；第 2 章主要由李学明和赵璐编写；第 3 章主要由赵琦编写；第 5 章主要由赵德斌和刘永欣编写；第 6 章主要由刘博和马丽娟编写。

中国民用航空中南地区管理局空中交通管制中心的钱旭、夏卫兵及深圳空管站航务部的艾国胜对本书部分内容的编写提供了悉心指导，保证了本书内容与"一线"实际所用的一致性。本书配套录音由 Todd Kendall（新西兰空中交通管制员、管制教员）和王万乐录制完成。中国民航大学空中交通管理学院学生吉瑞、高雪岩和冯佳怡对本书亦有贡献。在此一并表示衷心的感谢。

由于时间和编者水平有限，书中难免出现疏漏之处。我们衷心希望专家、同行和广大读者不吝指正，以完善本书。

编　者
2016 年 4 月

目　　录

第1章　基本运行程序 1
　　1.1　概述 1
　　1.2　字母 3
　　1.3　数字 5
　　1.4　标准单词和词组 12
　　1.5　呼号 18
　　1.6　通信的基本方法 20

第2章　机场管制——起飞前与起飞阶段 25
　　2.1　无线电检查 25
　　2.2　离场条件 27
　　2.3　重要机场情报 29
　　2.4　放行许可 30
　　2.5　推出开车 31
　　2.6　滑出 32
　　2.7　起飞 34

第3章　进近管制——离场阶段 36
　　3.1　雷达管制用语 36
　　3.2　离场指令 39
　　3.3　飞行活动通报 42

第4章　区域管制 45
　　4.1　高度信息 45
　　4.2　位置信息 47
　　4.3　航路等待 49
　　4.4　RVSM 运行与 SLOP 51
　　4.5　绕飞雷雨 52
　　4.6　航空器加入、穿越或离开航路 53

第5章　进近管制——进场阶段 55
　　5.1　进场及进近 55
　　5.2　雷达进近 59

第6章　机场管制——最后进近及着陆阶段 61
　　6.1　起落航线飞行 61
　　6.2　最后进近与着陆 63
　　6.3　滑入 64

I

  6.4 本场训练 ·· 66
第 7 章 紧急情况 ·· 69
  7.1 发布与认收 ·· 70
  7.2 处置与取消 ·· 71
"听录音"原文 ·· 73
  第 2 章 机场管制——起飞前与起飞阶段 ·· 73
  第 3 章 进近管制——离场阶段 ··· 74
  第 4 章 区域管制 ·· 75
  第 5 章 进近管制——进场阶段 ··· 76
  第 6 章 机场管制——最后进近及着陆阶段 ··· 77
  第 7 章 紧急情况 ·· 78
附录 A 国内常见航空公司的代码、话呼及公司名称 ·· 80
附录 B 国外常见航空公司的代码、话呼及公司名称 ·· 82
参考文献 ·· 84

第1章 基本运行程序

由于无线电陆空通话对航空安全的重要意义及其有别于日常交流的特殊性，国际民航组织对通话语言结构及内容制定了严格的标准。总体上，陆空通话标准术语具有严谨、简洁、无歧义等特点。

基本运行程序是所有管制员在指挥航空器时需要执行的通用程序，其中包括具有基础性、普遍性等特点的陆空通话。本章主要包括字母、数字、标准单词和词组、呼号及通信的基本方法等内容。

通过本章的学习，应达到以下学习目标：

> ❖ 掌握陆空通话的基本特点；
> ❖ 掌握字母、数字在陆空通话中的正确读音；
> ❖ 掌握标准单词和词组的正确发音及其含义；
> ❖ 掌握呼号的表达方法，以及常见航空公司三字代码的正确读音，注意区分相似呼号；
> ❖ 掌握通信的建立程序和一般原则；
> ❖ 理解正确使用标准陆空通话术语的重要性。

1.1 概述

1.1.1 通话基本要求

陆空通话使用送话器发送，采用按键通话（push-to-talk，PTT）方式。在同一通信频率内，任何时刻只应有一个电台发话，其他电台收听，否则容易出现波道卡阻的现象。

管制员在与驾驶员通话前应检查接收机音量是否设置在最佳音量位置，并确认波道中没有其他通信干扰。为避免歧义或误解，必须严格按照标准陆空通话的要求通话，且应注意以下方面：

（1）先想后说，应在发话之前想好说话内容，保证发话语句完整、流畅；
（2）先听后说，应避免干扰他人通话，确认他人通话完毕之后再发话；
（3）熟练掌握送话器使用技巧；
（4）发话速度适中，在发送需记录的信息时降低速率，使用英语通话时，每分钟发话不超过100个单词；
（5）发音清楚，保持通话音量平稳，语调正常；
（6）在通话中，数字前应稍作停顿，重读数字并以较慢语速发出，以便于理解；
（7）应避免使用"啊、哦"等犹豫不决的词；
（8）应在开始通话前按下发送开关，待发话完毕后再将其松开，以保证通话内容的完整性；

（9）应注意发话的语音、语调和节奏；
（10）一般情况下，每句管制指令中包含的管制内容不应超过三项，且应将相对重要的内容排列在管制指令的尾部。

1.1.2 通话结构

首次联系时应采用的通话结构为：

对方呼号+己方呼号（+通话内容）

例如：

> **P:** Dongfang Approach, CCA1356.
> **C:** CCA1356, Dongfang Approach.
>
> **P**：东方进近，CCA1356。
> **C**：CCA1356，东方进近。

首次通话以后的各次通话，管制员采用的通话结构一般为：

对方呼号+通话内容

例如：

> **C:** CES3662, climb to 6,000 meters.
> **P:** Climbing to 6,000 meters, CES3662.
>
> **C**：CES3362，上升到六千[①]。
> **P**：上升到六千，CES3662。

驾驶员采用的通话结构为：

对方呼号+己方呼号+通话内容

例如：

> **P:** Dongfang Tower, CSN6583, request push-back and start up.
> **C:** CSN6583, push-back and start up approved.
>
> **P**：东方塔台，CSN6583，请求推出开车。
> **C**：CSN6583，同意推出开车。

管制员确认驾驶员复诵的内容时可仅呼对方呼号。当管制员认为有必要时，可采用"read-back correct"具体确认。例如：

> **C:** CDG1152, taxi to holding point Runway 34 via Taxiways A, A7, Y and Z1.
> **P:** Taxi to holding point Runway 34 via Taxiways A, A7, Y and Z1, CDG1152.
> **C:** CDG1152, read-back correct.

---

① 为了强调高度指令的中文读法，本章涉及高度的中文指令均以读法显示。其他用阿拉伯数字表示的信息，其读法请参考本章 1.2 节和 1.3 节。

> C: CDG1152，沿滑行道 A，A7，Y 和 Z1 滑到 34 号跑道等待点。
> P: 沿滑行道 A，A7，Y 和 Z1 滑到 34 号跑道等待点，CDG1152。
> C: CDG1152，复诵正确。

1.2 字母

在无线电通话中，管制员和驾驶员都使用国际统一的标准字母，通过用单词为英语字母注音的方法来避免发音混淆。

1.2.1 听录音

表 1-1 为字母的标准读法，发音一栏中带下划线的部分应重读。请听录音并跟读。

表 1-1

字 母	单 词	发 音
A	Alpha	<u>AL</u> FAH
B	Bravo	<u>BRAH</u> VOH
C	Charlie	<u>CHAR</u> LEE or <u>SHAR</u> LEE
D	Delta	<u>DELL</u> TAH
E	Echo	<u>ECK</u> OH
F	Foxtrot	<u>FOKS</u> TROT
G	Golf	GOLF
H	Hotel	HO <u>TELL</u>
I	India	<u>IN</u> DEE AH
J	Juliett	<u>JEW</u> LEE <u>ETT</u>
K	Kilo	<u>KEY</u> LOH
L	Lima	<u>LEE</u> MAH
M	Mike	MIKE
N	November	NO <u>VEM</u> BER
O	Oscar	<u>OSS</u> CAH
P	Papa	PAH <u>PAH</u>
Q	Quebec	KEH <u>BECK</u>
R	Romeo	<u>ROW</u> ME OH
S	Sierra	SEE <u>AIR</u> RAH
T	Tango	<u>TANG</u> GO
U	Uniform	<u>YOU</u> NEE FORM or <u>OO</u> NEE FORM
V	Victor	<u>VIK</u> TAH

续表

字 母	单 词	发 音
W	Whiskey	WISS KEY
X	X-ray	ECKS RAY
Y	Yankee	YANG KEY
Z	Zulu	ZOO LOO

通话中，字母或字母组合可用来表示机场识别代码、信标台名称和航路点等，且应按无线电发音方式的发音规则读出。但需要注意的是，有些约定俗成的字母组合读法与此不同，如 ATIS，QNH，VOR，NDB 等，有的可按照一个单词读出，而有的则只需按照英语字母表的字母读法逐位读出。

1.2.2 机场识别代码的读法

机场识别代码按无线电发音方式逐位读出，如表 1-2 所示。

表 1-2

机场识别代码	英语读法	汉语读法
RJTY	ROMEO JULIETT TANGO YANKEE	ROMEO JULIETT TANGO YANKEE
ZBAA	ZULU BRAVO ALPHA ALPHA	ZULU BRAVO ALPHA ALPHA
EDDF	ECHO DELTA DELTA FOXTROT	ECHO DELTA DELTA FOXTROT

1.2.3 全向信标（VOR）台和无方向性信标（NDB）台的读法

英语读法为按照字母无线电发音读出该台识别码，汉语读法为按照航图中的地名读出，如表 1-3 所示。

表 1-3

VOR 和 NDB	英语读法	汉语读法
SIA	SIERRA INDIA ALPHA	西安
VYK	VICTOR YANKEE KILO	大王庄
SX	SIERRA X-RAY	南浔

对于 VOR 和 NDB 导航台名称相同，不建在一起且距离较远时，汉语读法应在台名后加 VOR 或 NDB，如表 1-4 所示。

表 1-4

VOR 和 NDB	英语读法	汉语读法
POU	PAPA OSCAR UNIFORM	平洲 VOR
XK	X-RAY KILO	平洲 NDB

1.2.4 航路点的读法

若航路点是五个英文字母,则中英文读法相同,约定俗成按照一个单词的英语发音读出。若航路点是由 P 和数字组成,英语按照无线电字母发音"PAPA"加数字的英语发音读出,汉语则按照字母"P"加数字的汉语发音读出,如表 1-5 所示。

表 1-5

航 路 点	英语读法	汉语读法
ANDIN	ANDIN	ANDIN
EPGAM	EPGAM	EPGAM
P23	PAPA TOO TREE	P 两三

1.2.5 航路的读法

航路由航路代号和编码组成,分别按照数字和字母的发音读出。航路代号前有"U""K""S"时,分别读作"upper""kopter"和"supersonic",表示高空、直升机和超音速航路。标准进离场航线的英语读法按照字母和数字的发音,后加"arrival"或"departure"读出,汉语读法为导航台名称+数字和字母的发音,后加"进场"或"离场",如表 1-6 所示。

表 1-6

航路、进离场航线	英语读法	汉语读法
G595	GOLF FIFE NIN-er FIFE	G 五九五 或 GOLF 五九五
A593	ALPHA FIFE NIN-er TREE	A 五九三 或 ALPHA 五九三
VYK-01A	VICTOR YANKEE KILO ZE-RO WUN ALPHA ARRIVAL	大王庄洞幺 ALPHA 进场

1.3 数字

1.3.1 🔊听录音

表 1-7 为数字的标准读法,请听录音并跟读。

表 1-7

数 字	英语读法	汉语读法
0	ZE-RO	洞
1	WUN	幺
2	TOO	两
3	TREE	三

续表

数　　字	英语读法	汉语读法
4	FOW-er	四
5	FIFE	五
6	SIX	六
7	SEV-en	拐
8	AIT	八
9	NIN-er	九
.	DAY-SEE-MAL	点
100	HUN-dred	百
1,000	TOU-SAND	千

你能发现有些数字的读法与普通英语里数字的读法不一致吗？发音不同的数字有：

通话中，数字组合可用来表示高度、时间、方向、二次雷达应答机编码、跑道、高度表设定值及频率等，且有其独特发音规则。数字组合的读法分为一般读法和特殊读法。

1.3.2　数字组合的一般读法

数字组合的英语读法通常按照数字的英语发音及顺序逐位读出；整百、整千或整千整百组合的数字通常读出数字，后面加上"hundred"或"tousand"。

数字组合的汉语读法一般按数字的汉语发音及顺序逐位读出；整百或整千组合的数字通常读出数字，后面加上"百"或"千"；整千整百组合的数字通常读出数字，千位后面加上"千"，百位后面通常不用加"百"；但一些约定俗成的数字例外，如用于机场区域内描述高度数据的数字"450"，可以读作"四五洞"或"四百五"，如表1-8所示。

表1-8

数　　字	英语读法	汉语读法
75	SEV-en FIFE	拐五
3,600	TREE TOU-SAND SIX HUN-dred	三千六
45,863	FOW-er FIFE AIT SIX TREE	四五八六三

1.3.3　数字组合的特殊读法

1. 高度

高度分为英制和公制，分别用"英尺"（feet）和"米"（meter）表示。我国高度层配备标准使用公制，在英文通话中需要加上单位"meters"，在中文通话中不加单位"米"，如表1-9所示。

表 1-9

高 度 层	英 语 读 法	汉 语 读 法
600 m	SIX HUN-dred METERS	六百
900 m	NIN-er HUN-dred METERS	九百
1,200 m	WUN TOU-SAND TOO HUN-dred METERS	一千二或 幺两
1,500 m	WUN TOU-SAND FIFE HUN-dred METERS	一千五或 幺五
1,800 m	WUN TOU-SAND AIT HUN-dred METERS	一千八或 幺八
2,100 m	TOO TOU-SAND WUN HUN-dred METERS	两幺
2,400 m	TOO TOU-SAND FOW-er HUN-dred METERS	两千四
2,700 m	TOO TOU-SAND SEV-en HUN-dred METERS	两千七或 两拐
3,000 m	TREE TOU-SAND METERS	三千
3,300 m	TREE TOU-SAND TREE HUN-dred METERS	三千三
3,600 m	TREE TOU-SAND SIX HUN-dred METERS	三千六
3,900 m	TREE TOU-SAND NIN-er HUN-dred METERS	三千九
4,200 m	FOW-er TOU-SAND TOO HUN-dred METERS	四千二或 四两
4,500 m	FOW-er TOU-SAND FIFE HUN-dred METERS	四千五
4,800 m	FOW-er TOU-SAND AIT HUN-dred METERS	四千八
5,100 m	FIFE TOU-SAND WUN HUN-dred METERS	五千一或 五幺
5,400 m	FIFE TOU-SAND FOW-er HUN-dred METERS	五千四
5,700 m	FIFE TOU-SAND SEV-en HUN-dred METERS	五千七或 五拐
6,000 m	SIX TOU-SAND METERS	六千
6,300 m	SIX TOU-SAND TREE HUN-dred METERS	六千三
6,600 m	SIX TOU-SAND SIX HUN-dred METERS	六千六
6,900 m	SIX TOU-SAND NIN-er HUN-dred METERS	六千九
7,200 m	SEV-en TOU-SAND TOO HUN-dred METERS	拐两
7,500 m	SEV-en TOU-SAND FIFE HUN-dred METERS	拐五
7,800 m	SEV-en TOU-SAND AIT HUN-dred METERS	拐八
8,100 m	AIT TOU-SAND WUN HUN-dred METERS	八千一或 八幺
8,400 m	AIT TOU-SAND FOW-er HUN-dred METERS	八千四
8,900 m	AIT TOU-SAND NIN-er HUN-dred METERS	八千九
9,200 m	NIN-er TOU-SAND TOO HUN-dred METERS	九千二
9,500 m	NIN-er TOU-SAND FIFE HUN-dred METERS	九千五

续表

高 度 层	英 语 读 法	汉 语 读 法
9,800 m	NIN-er TOU-SAND AIT HUN-dred METERS	九千八
10,100 m	WUN ZE-RO TOU-SAND WUN HUN-dred METERS or TEN TOUSAND WUN HUN-dred METERS	幺洞幺
10,400 m	WUN ZE-RO TOU-SAND FOW-er HUN-dred METERS or TEN TOUSAND FOW-er HUN-dred METERS①	幺洞四
10,700 m	WUN ZE-RO TOU-SAND SEV-en HUN-dred METERS or TEN TOUSAND SEV-en HUN-dred METERS	幺洞拐
11,000 m	WUN WUN TOU-SAND METERS or ELEVEN TOUSAND METERS②	幺幺洞
11,300 m	WUN WUN TOU-SAND TREE HUN-dred METERS or ELEVEN TOUSAND TREE HUN-dred METERS	幺幺三
11,600 m	WUN WUN TOU-SAND SIX HUN-dred METERS or ELEVEN TOUSAND SIX HUN-dred METERS	幺幺六
11,900 m	WUN WUN TOU-SAND NIN-er HUN-dred METERS or ELEVEN TOUSAND NIN-er HUN-dred METERS	幺幺九
12,200 m	WUN TOO TOU-SAND TOO HUN-dred METERS	幺两两
12,500 m	WUN TOO TOU-SAND FIFE HUN-dred METERS	幺两五
13,100 m	WUN TREE TOU-SAND WUN HUN-dred METERS	幺三幺
13,700 m	WUN TREE TOU-SAND SEV-en HUN-dred METERS	幺三拐
14,300 m	WUN FOW-er TOU-SAND TREE HUN-dred METERS	幺四三
14,900 m	WUN FOW-er TOU-SAND NIN-er HUN-dred METERS	幺四九

① 推荐使用前者。
② 推荐使用前者。

以标准大气压 1 013.2 hPa 为基准面，对符合英制高度层配备标准的高度，使用英语读法时，按照国际民航组织规定的发音，在"flight level"后逐位读出万位、千位和百位上的数字；使用汉语读法时，读出万位、千位和百位上的数字，高度层低于 10 000 英尺时，读作×千英尺，如表 1-10 所示。

表 1-10

高 度 层	英 语 读 法	汉 语 读 法
9,000 ft	FLIGHT LEVEL NIN-er ZE-RO	九千英尺
33,000 ft	FLIGHT LEVEL TREE TREE ZE-RO	三三洞

当高度指令涉及气压基准面转换时，管制员应在通话中指明新的气压基准面数值，在以后的通话中可省略气压基准面。使用英语读法时，对上升到 1 013.2 hPa 为基准面的高度，在高度数字后加上"on standard"，当以修正海平面气压为基准面时，在高度数字后加上"on QNH××××（数值）"；当以场面气压为基准面时，在高度数字后加上"on QFE××××（数值）"。

使用汉语读法时，对上升到以 1 013.2 hPa 为基准面的高度，在高度数字前加上"标准气压"；当以修正海平面气压为基准面时，在高度数字前加上"修正海压"，在高度数字后加上修正海压数值；当以场面气压为基准面时，在高度数字前加上"场压"，在高度数字后加上场压数值。例如：

C: HDA905, descend to 1,800 meters on QNH 1,011.

C： HDA905，下降到修正海压幺八，修正海压幺洞幺幺。

2. 时间

时间的读法一般只读出分，必要时（如可能引起混淆的情况下）应读出小时和分，如表 1-11 所示，时间精确到半分钟。

表 1-11

时　间	英 语 读 法	汉 语 读 法
0803（上午 8:03）	ZE-RO TREE　or　ZE-RO AIT ZE-RO TREE	洞三或洞八洞三
1300（下午 1:00）	ZE-RO ZE-RO　or　WUN TREE ZE-RO ZE-RO	整点或幺三洞洞

当驾驶员觉得必要时可与管制员进行时间检查（time check），这时通报时间的方式如表 1-12 所示。

表 1-12

时　间	英 语 读 法	汉 语 读 法
11:55:18	WUN WUN FIFE FIFE AND A HALF	幺幺五五三洞
11:55:38	WUN WUN FIFE SIX	幺幺五六

3. 气压

数字应逐位读出，如表 1-13 所示。

表 1-13

气　压	英 语 读 法	汉 语 读 法
QFE 1,003	QFE WUN ZE-RO ZE-RO TREE	场压幺洞洞三
QNH 1,000	QNH WUN ZE-RO ZE-RO ZE-RO	修正海压幺洞洞洞

4. 航向

航向后应跟三位数并逐位读出数值，如表 1-14 所示。

表 1-14

航　向	英 语 读 法	汉 语 读 法
100°	HEADING WUN ZE-RO ZE-RO	航向幺洞洞
005°	HEADING ZE-RO ZE-RO FIFE	航向洞洞五
360°	HEADING TREE SIX ZE-RO	航向三六洞

5. 速度

英语读法：逐位读出数值，后加速度单位；马赫数的读法为省略小数点前的0，读作"mach point ××"。

汉语读法：使用海里每小时（节）作为速度单位时，逐位读出数值，后不加单位；使用马赫数作为速度单位时，读作"马赫数点××"或"马赫数×点××"，如表1-15所示。

表1-15

速　　度	英　语　读　法	汉　语　读　法
280 knots	TOO AIT ZE-RO KNOTS	两八洞
M0.85	MACH POINT AIT FIFE	马赫数点八五

6. 风向风速

风向风速通常作为一个整体通报，风向后需加"degrees"（度），英语读法中风速的单位为knots（节），汉语读法中一般使用米每秒（m/s），如表1-16所示。

表1-16

风向风速	英　语　读　法	汉　语　读　法
160°,7 m/s, gusting 15 m/s	[SURFACE] WIND WUN SIX ZE-RO DEGREES SEV-en METERS PER SECOND GUSTING WUN FIFE METERS PER SECOND	地面风幺六洞度[①]，拐米每秒[②]，阵风幺五米每秒

7. 频率

频率应逐位读出，且英语读法应读出高频的单位，如表1-17所示。

表1-17

频　率	英　语　读　法	汉　语　读　法
121.45 MHz	WUN TOO WUN DAY-SEE-MAL FOW-er FIFE	幺两幺点四五
6,565 kHz	SIX FIFE SIX FIFE KILO HERTZ	六五六五

根据甚高频通信波道拥挤的状况，国际民航组织在某些地区将甚高频通信波道的频率间隔由25 kHz减小为8.33 kHz。使用8.33 kHz频率间隔的频率由六位数字组成，当最后两位均为"0"时，只需读出前四位，否则应逐位读出所有六位数字，如表1-18所示。

表1-18

波　　道	英　语　读　法	汉　语　读　法
118.000 MHz	WUN WUN AIT DAY-SEE-MAL ZE-RO	幺幺八点洞
118.010 MHz	WUN WUN AIT DAY-SEE-MAL ZE-RO WUN ZE-RO	幺幺八点洞幺洞
118.025 MHz	WUN WUN AIT DAY-SEE-MAL ZE-RO TOO FIFE	幺幺八点洞两五

---

① 在实际应用中，"度"常省略。
② 根据民用航空行业标准《空中交通无线电通话用语》（MH/T 4014—2003），风速单位"m/s"的汉语读法也可为"米秒"。

8. 跑道

跑道编号应按照数字的英语或汉语发音逐位读出。跑道编号后的英文字母"R""L"和"C",英语读作"right""left"和"center",汉语读作"右""左"和"中",如表1-19所示。

表 1-19

跑道号	英 语 读 法	汉 语 读 法
03	RUNWAY ZE-RO TREE	跑道洞三
08L	RUNWAY ZE-RO AIT LEFT	跑道洞八左

9. 距离

按照数字的一般读法读出,后面加上单位,如表1-20所示。

表 1-20

距 离	英 语 读 法	汉 语 读 法
18 n mile	WUN AIT MILES①	幺八海里
486 km	FOW-er AIT SIX KILOMETERS	四八六公里
400 km	FOW-er HUN-dred KILOMETERS	四百公里

10. 应答机编码

应答机编码按照数字的一般读法逐位读出,如表1-21所示。

表 1-21

应答机编码	英 语 读 法	汉 语 读 法
3213	SQUAWK TREE TOO WUN TREE	应答机三两幺三
5731	SQUAWK FIFE SEV-en TREE WUN	应答机五拐三幺

11. 航空器机型

航空器机型通常按照航空器制造商注册名加机型的方式读出,如表1-22所示。

表 1-22

机 型	英 语 读 法	汉 语 读 法
B737-300	BOEING SEV-en TREE SEV-en TREE HUN-dred	波音七三七三百
A340	AIRBUS TREE FOW-er ZE-RO	空客三四零
MA60	MODERN ARK SIX ZE-RO	新舟六零
EMB145	EMB WUN FOW-er FIFE	EMB 幺四五
TU-204	TUPOLEV TOO ZE-RO FOW-er	图两洞四

---

① 在陆空通话中,表示距离的单位是海里(n mile),英语读法约定俗成读作"mile"。

机 型	英 语 读 法	汉 语 读 法
D-328	DORNIER TREE TOO AIT	道尼尔三两八
CRJ-200	CRJ TOO HUN-red	CRJ 两百

12. 气象

有关气象方面的数字的读法，如能见度和跑道视程按照表 1-23 所示读出。

表 1-23

气 象	英 语 读 法	汉 语 读 法
能见度 2 000	VISIBILITY TOO TOU-SAND METERS	能见度两千米
跑道视程 700	RUNWAY VISUAL RANGE (or RVR) SEV-en HUN-dred METERS	跑道视程七百米

1.4 标准单词和词组

下列标准单词在通话中具有特定的含义。

（1）acknowledge（请认收）——Let me know that you have received and understood this message.（向我表示你已经收到并理解该电报。）

例如：

> **C:** CHB6263, do not acknowledge my further transmissions.
>
> **C：** CHB6263，请不要认收以下通话。

（2）affirm（是的）——Yes.（是的。）

例如：

> **C:** CSN6412, are you ready for immediate departure?
> **P:** Affirm, CSN6412.
>
> **C：** CSN6412，能立即起飞吗？
> **P：** 是的，CSN6412。

（3）approved（同意）——Permission for proposed action granted.（批准所申请的行动。）

例如：

> **P:** Dongfang Ground, UAL7610, request push-back and start up.
> **C:** UAL7610, push-back and start up approved.
>
> **P：** 东方地面，UAL7610，请求推出开车。
> **C：** UAL7610，同意推出开车。

（4）break（还有）——I hereby indicate the separation between portions of the message to be used where there is no clear distinction between the text and other portions of the message.（表示电报各部分的间断；用于电文与电报的其他部分无明显区别的情况。如果信息的各个部分之间没有明显的区别可以使用该词作为信息各部分之间的间隔标志。）

例如：

> **C:** ACA030, taxi to holding point A1, Runway 18R, break, taxiway centerline lighting unserviceable.
> **P:** Roger, ACA030.
>
> **C:** ACA030，滑到A1等待点，跑道18右，还有，滑行道中央灯光故障。
> **P:** 收到，ACA030。

（5）break break（另外）——I hereby indicate the separation between messages transmitted to different aircrafts in a very busy environment.（表示在非常繁忙的情况下，发布给不同航空器的电报之间的间断。）

例如：

> **C:** AAL186, descend immediately to 6,900 meters, break break, CCA1421, climb immediately to 7,500 meters.
>
> **C:** AAL186，立即下降到六千九，另外，CCA1421，立即上升到拐五。

（6）cancel（取消）——Annul the previously transmitted clearance.（废除此前所发布的许可。）

例如：

> **C:** THY021, hold position, cancel take-off, I say again, cancel take-off, vehicle crossing the runway.
>
> **C:** THY021，原地等待，取消起飞，重复一遍，取消起飞，有车辆穿越跑道。

（7）check（检查）——Examine a system or procedure, and no answer is normally expected.（检查系统或程序，且通常不回答。）

例如：

> **C:** KAL5802, check your transmitter and give me a long call.
>
> **C:** KAL5802，检查你的发射机并给我一长呼。

（8）cleared（可以）——Authorized to proceed under the conditions specified.（批准按指定条件前行。）

例如：

> C: JAL020, wind calm, Runway 18, cleared for take-off.
>
> C：JAL020，静风，跑道 18，可以起飞。

（9）confirm（证实）——I request verification of (clearance, instruction, action, information)（我请求核实：许可、指令、行动和信息。）

例如：

> C: SWR197, confirm squawk 3352.
>
> C：SWR197，证实应答机编码 3352。

（10）contact（联系）——Establish communications with…（与……建立通信。）

例如：

> C: SIA805, contact Dongfang Tower on 118.8.
>
> C：SIA805，联系东方塔台 118.8。

（11）correct（正确）——True or accurate.（真实的或准确的。）

例如：

> C: UAE307, read-back correct.
>
> C：UAE307，复诵正确。

（12）correction（更正）——An error has been made in this transmission (or message indicated). The correct version is…（本电报出了一个错误，或所发布的信息本身是错的，正确的内容应当是……）

例如：

> C: THA615, climb to 7,500 meters, correction, climb to 7,800 meters.
>
> C：THA615，上升到拐五，更正，上升到拐八。

（13）disregard（作废）——Ignore.（忽视。）

例如：

> C: MAS361, descend to…, disregard, maintain present level.
>
> C：MAS361，下降到……，作废，保持现在高度。

（14）How do you read?（听我信号怎样？）——What is the readability of my transmission?（我所发电报的清晰度如何？）

例如：

> **P:** Dongfang Tower, MGL224, how do you read?
>
> **P:** 东方塔台，MGL224，听我信号怎样？

（15）I say again（我重复一遍）——I repeat for clarity or emphasis.（为了表示澄清或强调，我重复一遍。）

例如：

> **C:** PAL359, hold position, cancel take-off, I say again, cancel take-off, due vehicle on the runway.
>
> **C：** PAL359，原地等待，取消起飞，重复一遍，取消起飞，跑道上有车辆。

（16）maintain（保持）——Continue in accordance with the condition(s) specified or in its literal sense, e.g. "Maintain VFR".（依照指定条件继续或按字面意义，如"保持 VFR"。）

例如：

> **C:** CHH7265, maintain 5,400 meters, expect descent after VYK.
> **P:** Maintaining 5,400 meters, CHH7265.
>
> **C：** CHH7265，保持五千四，预计过大王庄后下降。
> **P：** 保持五千四，CHH7265。

（17）monitor（守听）——Listen out on (frequency).（留心听某个频率。）

例如：

> **C:** PIA853, monitor ATIS 123.25.
>
> **C：** PIA853，123.25 上守听通播。

（18）negative（不、不同意、不对或不能）——No or Permission not granted or That is not correct or Not capable.（并非如此，或不允许，或不对，或不能。）

例如：

> **C:** QTR895, descend to 8,400 meters.
> **P:** Descending to 8,100 meters, QTR895.
> **C:** QTR895, negative, descend to 8,400 meters.
> **P:** Descending to 8,400 meters, QTR895.
>
> **C：** QTR895，下降到八千四。
> **P：** 下降到八千一，QTR895。
> **C：** QTR895，不对，下降到八千四。
> **P：** 下降到八千四，QTR895。

（19）out（完毕）——This exchange of transmissions is ended and no response is expected.（本次通话已经结束，并且你不需要作出回答。）

"out"通常不用于VHF通信中。

（20）over（请回答）——My transmission is ended and I expect a response from you.（我发话完毕，并希望你回答。）

"over"通常不用于VHF通信中。

（21）read back（请复诵）——Repeat all, or the specified part of this message back to me exactly as received.（请向我准确地重复本电报所有或部分内容。）

例如：

> C: AMU007, descend to 2,700 meters on QNH 1,010.
> P: Descending to 2,700 meters, AMU007.
> C: AMU007, please read back QNH.
>
> C：AMU007，下降到修正海压两拐，修正海压幺洞幺洞。
> P：下降到修正海压两拐，AMU007。
> C：AMU007，请复诵修正海压。

（22）recleared（重新许可）——A change has been made to your last clearance and this new clearance supersedes your previous clearance or part thereof.（此前发布给你的许可已经变更，这一新的许可将取代刚才的许可或其中部分内容。）

例如：

> C: OKA2851, recleared to Dongfang via KNOCK J1 BRAVO.
>
> C：OKA2851，重新许可经由KNOCK J1 BRAVO去往东方机场。

（23）report（报告）——Pass me the following information...（向我报告下列信息……）

例如：

> C: HXA2674, report speed.
> P: Speed 250 knots, HXA2674.
>
> C：HXA2674，报告速度。
> P：速度250，HXA2674。

（24）request（请求）——I should like to know..., or I wish to obtain...（我希望知道……或我希望得到……）

例如：

> P: Dongfang Ground, HVN513, request taxi to Runway 36L.
>
> P：东方地面，HVN513，请求滑行到36左跑道。

(25) roger（收到）——I have received all of your last transmission.（我已经收到了你刚才的发话。）

在任何情况下，不得采用"roger"来回答要求复诵或要求回答"是"或"否"的问题。

例如：

> **C:** CAL512, a preceding aircraft reported wind shear on final.
> **P:** Roger, CAL512.
>
> **C**：CAL512，前机报告五边有风切变。
> **P**：收到，CAL512。

(26) say again（再说或重复一遍）——Repeat all, or the following part of your last transmission.（请重复你刚才发话的所有内容或下列部分。）

例如：

> **P:** Dongfang Tower, …
> **C:** Station calling Tower, say again your call sign.
> **P:** Dongfang Tower, AFL201.
>
> **P**：东方塔台，……
> **C**：呼叫塔台的电台，重复一下你的呼号。
> **P**：东方塔台，AFL201。

(27) speak slower（讲慢点）——Reduce your rate of speech.（请降低你的语速。）

例如：

> **C:** FIN052, Dongfang Tower, speak slower.
>
> **C**：FIN052，东方塔台，请讲慢点。

(28) stand by（稍等或等待）——Wait and I will call you.（请等候，我将呼叫你。）

例如：

> **P:** Dongfang Tower, AAR336, Gate 15, Information C, request push-back.
> **C:** AAR336, stand by.
> **P:** Standing by, AAR336.
>
> **P**：东方塔台，AAR336，15号位，通播C，请求推出。
> **C**：AAR336，稍等。
> **P**：稍等，AAR336。

（29）unable（不能）——I cannot comply with your request, instruction, or clearance. （我不能按照你的请求、指令或许可执行。）

unable 后通常应跟不能执行的原因。

例如：

> C: CES5186, climb to 8,900 meters, expedite until passing 8,400 meters.
> P: Unable to expedite climb due weight, CES5186.
>
> C：CES5186，上升到八千九，快速通过八千四。
> P：由于重量大，不能快速通过八千四，CES5186。

（30）wilco（照办）——Abbreviation for "will comply". I understand your message and will comply with it. （"将照办"的缩略语。我已经明白了你的电报并将按照该电报执行。）

例如：

> C: EVA716, report over ZHO.
> P: Wilco, EVA716.
>
> C：EVA716，到达周口报告。
> P：照办，EVA716。

（31）words twice（讲两遍）—— ① As a request: Communication is difficult. Please send every word or group of words twice. [对于申请来说：因为通信困难，请把每个词（组）发送两遍。] ② As information: Since communication is difficult, every word or group of words in this message will be sent twice. [对于信息来说：因为通信困难，该电报的每个词（组）将被发送两遍。]

例如：

> C: ALK504, here is your ATC clearance, words twice.
> P: Ready to copy, ALK504.
>
> C：ALK504，你的放行许可，讲两遍。
> P：准备抄收，ALK504。

1.5 呼号

1.5.1 管制单位呼号

管制单位一般用地名加后缀的方式作为其呼号，后缀表明提供何种服务或单位类型，如表 1-24 所示。

表 1-24

管制或服务单位	呼号后缀
area control center（区域管制中心）	control（区域）
radar（雷达①）	radar（雷达）
approach control（进近管制）	approach（进近）
approach control radar arrival（进场雷达管制）	arrival（进场）
approach control radar departure（离场雷达管制）	departure（离场）
aerodrome control（机场管制）	tower（塔台）
surface movement control（地面活动管制）	ground（地面）
clearance delivery（放行许可发布）	delivery（放行）
precision approach radar（精密进近雷达）	precision（精密）
flight information service（飞行情报服务）	information（情报）
apron control/management service（机坪管制或管理服务）	apron（机坪）
company dispatch（公司签派）	dispatch（签派）

① 此为通用雷达。

1.5.2 航空器呼号

航空器呼号分为三类，其中某些形式的呼号有简呼形式。

（1）航空器的注册号：注册号字母和数字应按照字母和数字的标准发音逐位读出。有时以航空器制造厂商或航空器名作为注册号字母的前缀，制造厂商或航空器名则按照英语发音习惯或翻译的汉语读出。例如：

> G-ABCD: GOLF ALPHA BRAVO CHARLIE DELTA
> Cessna G-ABCD: CESSNA GOLF ALPHA BRAVO CHARLIE DELTA

（2）航空器经营人的无线电呼号加航空器注册号的最后四位字母：航空器经营人呼号的英语发音按照 ICAO 指定的无线电呼号读出，中国航空公司呼号的汉语发音按照中国民航规定的呼号读出；注册号的字母全部按照字母的英语标准发音逐位读出；数字应分别按照数字的英语、汉语标准发音逐位读出。例如：

> BAW BHWC: SPEEDBIRD BRAVO HOTEL WHISKEY CHARLIE

（3）航空器经营人的无线电呼号加航班号：航空器经营人呼号的英语发音按照 ICAO 指定的无线电呼号读出，中国航空公司呼号汉语发音按照中国民航规定的呼号读出；航班号的字母全部按照字母的英语标准发音逐位读出；数字应按照数字的英语、汉语标准发音逐位读出。例如：

> BAW038: SPEEDBIRD ZE-RO TREE AIT
> CES7255: CHINA EASTERN SEV-en TOO FIFE FIFE（英语读法） or 东方拐两五五（汉语读法）

在建立满意的双向通信联系之后，在无任何混淆产生的情况下，可以使用航空器的简呼，且先应由管制员简呼航空器，航空器才能以简呼作为自呼。上述航空器呼号的缩减形式如下：

（1）航空器注册号中第一个和至少最后两个字母，如：G-CD 或 Cessna G-CD；
（2）航空器经营人的无线电呼号加航空器注册号中至少最后两个字母，如 BAW WC；
（3）航空器经营人的无线电呼号加航班号，无缩减形式，如 BAW038 无简呼。

当由于存在相似呼号而可能产生混淆时，管制单位可临时指示航空器改变呼号形式。例如：

> C: CSN3107, change your call sign to B2456, similar call sign.
> P: Change call sign to B2456, CSN3107.
>   (A moment later)
> C: B2456, revert to flight plan call sign CSN3107 at NSH.
>
> C：CSN3107，将你的呼号改为 B2456，有相似呼号。
> P：将呼号改为 B2456，CSN3107。
>   （稍后）
> C：B2456，在宁陕恢复到飞行计划中的呼号 CSN3107。

对于 A380 机型，当机组与管制单位首次建立联系时，驾驶员必须在其航班呼号后增加"super"一词。当航空器尾流等级为重型时，在与塔台和进近管制员首次联系时应在其呼号后加上"重型"（heavy）一词。例如：

> P: Dongfang Tower, UAL089, heavy, request taxi.
>
> P：东方塔台，UAL089，重型，请求滑行。

1.6 通信的基本方法

1.6.1 通信的建立

初次建立联系时，航空器应使用航空器和管制单位的全称。例如：

> P: Shanghai Approach, G-ABCD.
> C: G-ABCD, Shanghai Approach.
>
> P：上海进近，G-ABCD。
> C：G-ABCD，上海进近。

如果地面电台或某一航空器需要广播信息或情报时，可以在信息或情报前加上"All stations"（全体注意）。例如：

> **P:** All stations, G-CDAB, southbound CHO VOR to Dongfang, leaving 6,000 meters now, descending to 4,500 meters.
>
> **P:** 全体注意，G-CDAB，从 CHO VOR 往南去东方，现在离开六千，下降到四千五。

在不确定信息是否接收正确时，可要求重复所发送信息的部分或全部内容，采用表 1-25 中的用语。

表 1-25

用 语	含 义
say again（重复）	repeat entire message（重复完整信息）
say again … (item)（重复……）	repeat specific item（重复特定信息项）
say again all before …（重复……之前）	repeat that part of the message before the first satisfactorily received word（重复第一个接收清楚单词之前的那部分信息）
say again all after …（重复……之后）	repeat that part of the message after the last satisfactorily received word（重复最后一个接收清楚单词之后的那部分信息）
say again all between … and …（重复……和……之间）	repeat that part of the message between two satisfactorily received words（重复在两个接收清楚单词之间的那部分信息）

例如：

> **C:** VIR7937, cleared to Hong Kong via flight planned route, RENOB8B Departure, initial climb to 900 meters on QNH 1,014, maintain 10,100 meters on standard, squawk 3475.
>
> **P:** Dongfang Delivery, say again all after QNH 1,014.
>
> **C:** VIR7937, maintain 10,100 meters on standard, squawk 3475.
>
> **P:** Cleared to Hong Kong via flight planned route, RENOB8B Departure, initial climb to 900 meters on QNH 1,014, maintain 10,100 meters on standard, squawk 3475, VIR7937.
>
> **C：** VIR7937，可以经飞行计划航路飞往香港，RENOB8B 离场，起始爬升高度九百，修正海压幺洞幺四，在航路上保持标准气压幺洞幺巡航，应答机 3475。
>
> **P：** 东方放行，请重复 QNH 幺洞幺四之后的信息。
>
> **C：** VIR7937，在航路上保持标准气压幺洞幺巡航，应答机 3475。
>
> **P：** 可以经飞行计划航路飞往香港，RENOB8B 离场，起始爬升高度九百，修正海压幺洞幺四，在航路上保持标准气压幺洞幺巡航，应答机 3475，VIR7937。

如果被呼叫单位不能确定谁呼叫自己，被呼叫单位可要求对方重复呼号直至建立联系。例如：

> **C:** Station calling Beijing Ground, say again your call sign.
>
> **C：** 哪个呼叫北京地面，请重复呼号。

如果管制员或驾驶员在发布指令或报告的过程中出现错误并立即更正，应使用"correction"（更正），重复更正后的正确部分。如果需要通过重复全部指令或报告才能更好地更正错误，可使用"correction I say again"（更正，我重复一遍）。例如：

> C: BAW038, cleared to Beijing via flight planned route, NOMAD11D Departure, initial climb to 900 meters on QNH 1,010, request level change en route, squawk 5310. Correction I say again, BAW038, cleared to Beijing via flight planned route, NOMAD11D Departure, initial climb to 900 meters on QNH 1,014, request level change en route, squawk 5310.
>
> P: Cleared to Beijing via flight planned route, NOMAD11D Departure, initial climb to 900 meters on QNH 1,014, request level change en route, squawk 5310, BAW038.
>
> C: BAW038, read-back correct.
>
> C：BAW038，可以经飞行计划航路飞往北京，NOMAD11D 离场，起始爬升高度九百，修正海压幺洞幺洞，在航路上申请改变高度，应答机 5310。更正，我重复一遍，BAW038，可以经飞行计划航路飞往北京，NOMAD11D 离场，起始爬升高度九百，修正海压幺洞幺四，在航路上申请改变高度，应答机 5310。
>
> P：可以经飞行计划航路飞往北京，NOMAD11D 离场，起始爬升高度九百，修正海压幺洞幺四，在航路上申请改变高度，应答机 5310，BAW038。
>
> C：BAW038，复诵正确。

当管制员或驾驶员认为对方接收可能有困难或有必要时，应重复通话中的重要内容，可使用"I say again"。例如：

> P: Shanghai Approach, QFA301, 2,700 meters maintaining, I say again, 2,700 meters maintaining, engine losing power, engine losing power.
>
> P：上海进近，QFA301，两拐保持，我重复一遍，两拐保持，发动机失去推力，发动机失去推力。

1.6.2 许可的发布与复诵要求

驾驶员应向管制员复诵通过话音传送的 ATC 放行许可和指令中涉及安全的部分。具体来说，应复诵下列内容：

（1）空中交通管制航路放行许可；

（2）进入跑道、起飞、着陆、跑道外等待、穿越跑道和沿正在使用跑道的反方向滑行的许可和指令；

（3）正在使用的跑道、高度表拨正值、二次监视雷达（SSR）编码、高度指令、航向与速度指令和空中交通管制员发布的或 ATIS 广播包含的过渡高度层。

对于其他许可和指令，包括附加条件许可，驾驶员复诵和认收的方式应能清楚表明，自己已理解并将遵照执行这些许可和指令。

驾驶员应以呼号终止复诵。管制员必须监听驾驶员复诵。在肯定驾驶员复诵的内容正确时，可仅呼叫对方呼号。如果驾驶员复诵的指令或许可错误，管制员应明确发送"negative"（错误）后跟更正的内容。

如果对驾驶员能否遵照执行许可和指令有疑问,管制员在许可和指令后可加短语"if unable, advise"(如果不行,通知我),随后发布其他替换指令。任何时候,如果驾驶员认为不能遵照执行接收到的许可和指令,应使用短语"unable"(无法执行),并告知原因。

附加条件用语,如"在航空器着陆之后"或"在航空器起飞之后",不应发布给对使用跑道有影响的活动,除非有关管制员或驾驶员能看见相关航空器或车辆。收到具有附加条件许可的航空器需要正确识别相关航空器或车辆。附加条件许可发布的格式如下:

(1) identification（识别标志）;
(2) the condition（条件）;
(3) the clearance（许可）;
(4) brief reiteration of the condition（条件的简要重复）。

例如:

> C: CSS6878, behind the landing airbus on short final, line up behind.
> P: Line up behind the landing airbus on short final, CSS6878.
>
> C：CSS6878,在短五边上的空客落地后进跑道。
> P：在短五边上的空客落地后进跑道,CSS6878。

在发布应马上执行的指令,表明如果不执行指令将会造成严重的飞行冲突时,应使用"immediately"(立即)。在其他情况下,可使用"commence (action) now"(现在开始执行……)。

> C: CES5186, go around immediately, aircraft on runway.
>
> C：CES5186,立即复飞,跑道上有飞机。

1.6.3 通信的移交

当航空器需要从一个无线电频率转换到另一个频率时,管制员应通知驾驶员转换频率。例如:

> C: SIA5188, contact Dongfang Control on 127.5.
> P: 127.5, SIA5188.
>
> C：SIA5188,联系东方区域 127.5。
> P：127.5,SIA5188。

如果管制单位没有通知,驾驶员应在转换频率之前提醒管制员。例如:

> P: Dongfang Control, YZR7968, request change to 127.5.
> C: YZR7968, Dongfang Control, frequency change approved.
>
> P：东方区域,YZR7968,请求转换频率 127.5。

C：YZR7968，东方区域，同意转换频率。

当其他空中交通服务单位需要和航空器进一步通话时，可指示航空器"stand by (frequency)"（在……频率上守听），此时管制单位应首先与航空器联系。例如：

C: KOR152, stand by for Dongfang Tower 118.1.
P: 118.1, KOR152.

C：KOR152，在东方塔台 118.1 上等待。
P：118.1，KOR152。

指示航空器守听某广播频率时，应使用"monitor（frequency）"。例如：

C: AIC348, Pudong Ground, monitor ATIS 127.85.
P: 127.85, AIC348.

C：AIC348，浦东地面，在 127.85 上守听通播。
P：127.85，AIC348。

第 2 章　机场管制——起飞前与起飞阶段

起飞前与起飞阶段主要包括航空器放行许可、推出、开车、滑行、进跑道和起飞等。此阶段所涉及的通话术语相对丰富、繁杂。特别是在停机位、机坪及滑行道上所使用的术语，往往要根据实际情景进行语言组织。此外，各类重要机场信息的通报也是此阶段术语中的重要内容。

通过本章的学习，应达到以下学习目标：

- ❖ 掌握无线电检查程序和用语；
- ❖ 掌握放行许可的格式和用语；
- ❖ 掌握推出、开车、滑行、进跑道等指令，以及起飞许可的格式和用语；
- ❖ 掌握重要信息通报的格式和内容；
- ❖ 理解离场条件的内容；
- ❖ 了解机场通播的各项内容及用语。

2.1　无线电检查

管制员或驾驶员认为必要时，可利用无线电检查程序，检查其无线电设备是否工作正常。

2.1.1　单词与词组

readability	清晰程度
transmission	发话
transmitter	发射机
box	无线电收发机
loud and clear	声音洪亮清楚
cut in and out	时断时续
loud background whistle	背景音刺耳
short count	短数
long call	长呼

2.1.2　🔊听录音

2.1.3 典型格式与范例

> **1. 无线电检查程序应采用的形式**
> （1） 对方电台呼号；
> （2） 己方电台呼号；
> （3） 无线电检查（radio check）；
> （4） 使用的频率。
>
> **2. 无线电检查回答应按照的形式**
> （1） 对方电台呼号；
> （2） 己方电台呼号；
> （3） 所发射信号的质量（readability）。

发射信号的质量如表 2-1 所示。

表 2-1[①]

通 话 质 量	英 语 描 述	汉 语 描 述
unreadable（不清楚）	WUN	一个
readable now and then（可断续听到）	TOO	两个
readable but with difficulty（能听清但很困难）	TREE	三个
readable（清楚）	FOW-er	四个
perfectly readable（非常清晰）	FIFE	五个

信号检查的英语通话按照 1.3 节数字的标准发音读出；汉语通话按照"信号一（两、三、四、五）个"读出。

范例：

(1) P: Dongfang Ground, ABW422, **radio check on 121.5. How do you read me?**
C: ABW422, Dongfang Ground, **I read you 5.**

P：东方地面，ABW422，无线电检查 121.5，听我信号怎样？
C：ABW422，东方地面，我听你五个。

(2) P: Beijing Tower, KZR888, radio check on 118.55.

C: **Station calling Beijing Tower, say again your call sign**, you are unreadable.
   (or)
C: KZR888, Beijing Tower, **reading you 3**, loud background whistle.

P：北京塔台，KZR888，无线电检查 118.55。
C：哪架飞机叫北京塔台，请重复呼号，信号不清楚。
（或）
C：KZR888，北京塔台，听你三个，背景音刺耳。

---

① 此表参考民用航空行业标准《空中交通无线电通话用语》（MH/T 4014—2003）。

2.2 离场条件

2.2.1 离场条件

在航空器离场前，需要了解天气、使用跑道及高度表拨正值等信息，此类信息一般可由机场通播获取，如机场不提供机场通播，驾驶员可在请求开车之前向管制员请求离场条件。

2.2.1.1 单词与词组

surface wind	地面风
dew point	露点
gusting	阵风
visibility	能见度
plus	正的
minus	负的
work in progress	正在施工
braking action	刹车效应

2.2.1.2 🔊 听录音

2.2.1.3 典型格式与范例

（1）航空器呼号（call sign）；
（2）起飞跑道（runway-in-use）；
（3）风向、风速（wind speed, wind direction）；
（4）高度表拨正值（QNH/QFE）；
（5）温度、露点（temperature, dew point）；
（6）能见度或跑道视程（visibility/RVR）。

范例：

P: Dongfang Ground, CQH345, IFR to Shanghai, request departure information.
C: CQH345, departure Runway 32, wind 290 degrees 4 knots, QNH 1,022, temperature minus 2, dew point minus 3, RVR 550 meters, time 27.
P: Runway 32, QNH 1,022, will call for start up, CQH345.

P：东方地面，CQH345，仪表飞行规则，目的地上海，请求离场条件。
C：CQH345，离场跑道 32，地面风 290 度，4 节，修正海压 1 022，温度负 2，露点负 3，跑道视程 550 米，时间 27。
P：跑道 32，修正海压 1 022，将请求开车，CQH345。

2.2.2 机场通播

通播（ATIS）是在繁忙机场自动连续播放的情报服务。ATIS 通常在一个单独的无线电频率上进行广播，一般每小时更新一次，天气变化迅速时也可随时更新，依次以字母代码 A，B，

C，…，Z 表示，并按照 ICAO 标准读法读出。根据需要，通播可分为离场通播、进场通播和进离场通播。

2.2.2.1　单词与词组

designator	代码
transition level	过渡高度层
transition altitude	过渡高度
ceiling	云底高
hectopascal	百帕
millibar	毫巴

2.2.2.2　🔊 听录音

2.2.2.3　典型格式与范例

> （1）机场名称；
> （2）通播代码；
> （3）发布时间；
> （4）使用跑道；
> （5）重要的跑道道面情况；
> （6）地面风向风速；
> （7）能见度、跑道视程；
> （8）现行天气报告；
> （9）大气温度、露点、高度表拨正值；
> （10）趋势型着陆天气预报；
> （11）其他必要的飞行情报及自动情报服务的信息。

范例：

Beijing capital international airport Information K. 0700UTC. Main landing Runway 36R, ILS approach, main departure Runway 36L. Runway surface wet, braking action poor. Wind 280 degrees, 6 m/s, gusting to 12 m/s. Visibility 4,000 meters, intermittent light rain, overcast, ceiling 900 meters. Temperature 23, dew point 22. QNH 1,006. Taxiway L closed. Advise on initial contact you have Information K.

北京首都国际机场情报通播 K，0700 世界协调时，主着陆使用跑道 36 右，ILS 进近，主起飞跑道 36 左。跑道道面湿，刹车效应差。风向 280 度，6 米每秒，阵风 12 米每秒。能见度 4 000 米，间断小雨，阴天，云底高 900 米。温度 23，露点 22。修正海压 1 006。滑行道 L 关闭。首次与管制员联络时报告您已收到通播 K。

2.3 重要机场情报

重要机场情报是有关活动区及其相关设施的信息，这些信息对于航空器的安全运行具有十分重要的意义。在航空器开车前或滑行前，以及开始最后进近前，除非已知航空器已从其他来源获取部分或全部的机场情报，否则，应尽可能向其提供重要机场情报。重要机场情报包括：活动区内及其邻近区域内进行的施工或维修工程；跑道上、滑行道上或停机坪上道面不平或破损情况（不管是否已做出标记）；跑道上、滑行道上或停机坪上有积雪、雪浆或结冰和积水的情况及其附近雪堆的情况；其他临时危害，包括地面上及空中的鸟类；机场灯光系统部分或全部不工作或故障情况；其他相关信息。

2.3.1 单词与词组

construction work	施工
work in progress	正在施工
slush	雪浆
snow bank	雪堆
unserviceable/inoperative/unavailable	不工作的、无用的
braking action (good, medium, poor)	刹车效应（好，中，差）
flock of birds	鸟群
water patches	块状积水
vehicle	车辆
wind shear	风切变

2.3.2 🔊听录音

2.3.3 范例

(1) **C:** DKH1022, **caution construction work** adjacent to Gate 37.

C：DKH1022，注意 37 号桥附近有施工。

(2) **C:** SBI874, **caution work in progress** ahead south side of Taxiway A.

C：SBI874，注意前方滑行道 A 南侧正在施工。

(3) **C:** TBA9815, caution taxiway center line **lighting unserviceable**.

C：TBA9815，注意滑行道中线灯不可用。

(4) **C:** EPA6218, caution VASIS Runway 27 unserviceable.

C：EPA6218，注意 27 号跑道 VASIS 系统不可用。

(5) **C:** CSC9988, caution large **flock of birds** north of Runway 27 near main taxiway.

C：CSC9988，注意 27 号跑道北侧主滑附近有大群鸟活动。

(6)	C: CHH7265, caution ILS Runway 09 unserviceable.		C：CHH7265，注意 09 号跑道 ILS 不可用。
(7)	C: ACA030, caution runway conditions 09: available width 32 meters, covered with thin patches of ice, **braking action** poor, snow up to 30 centimeters along edge.		C：ACA030，注意 09 号跑道条件：可用宽度 32 米，薄积冰覆盖，刹车效应差，边缘积雪 30 厘米。

2.4 放行许可

驾驶员在收到离场条件或离场 ATIS 之后，通常在开车前 5~10 分钟向地面或放行单位请求放行许可。

当驾驶员需要记录，同时为避免无谓的重复，管制员应缓慢地、清楚地发布许可。放行许可宜在开车前发布给驾驶员，不应在驾驶员对正跑道和实施起飞动作时发布放行许可。

放行许可抄收好后，驾驶员必须复诵许可内容，在被证实准确无误后请求推出开车。

2.4.1 单词与词组

flight planned route	计划航路
valid	有效
squawk	（调置）应答机
en route	航路上

2.4.2 听录音

2.4.3 典型格式与范例

（1）航空器呼号；
（2）许可界限（通常指目的地机场）；
（3）飞行的航路或航线；
（4）指定的标准仪表离场代号（没有代号的情况除外）；
（5）飞行高度；
（6）应答机编码；
（7）其他必要指令或信息，如转频的指令。

范例：

(1)	P: Pudong Delivery, CCA102, destination Beijing with Information B, request ATC clearance. C: CCA102, Information B is valid, **cleared to Beijing via flight planned route**, runway-	P：浦东放行，CCA102，目的地北京，通播 B，请求放行许可。 C：CCA102，通播 B 有效，可以沿计划航路放行至北京，使用跑道 17，PIKAS11D

in-use 17, PIKAS11D, **initial climb to** 900 meters on QNH 1,011, **request level change for 9,800 meters en route**, squawk 5310. Contact Approach on 123.8 when airborne.
P: Cleared to Beijing via flight planned route, runway-in-use 17, PIKAS11D, initial climb to 900 meters on QNH 1,011, request level change for 9,800 meters en route, squawk 5310, contact Approach on 123.8 when airborne, CCA102.
C: CCA102 read-back correct, contact Ground on 121.65, good day.

(2) **P:** Dalian Ground, AAR3365, destination Seoul with Information G, request ATC clearance.
C: AAR3365, Information G is valid, cleared to Seoul via flight planned route, **initial altitude** 900 meters on QNH 998, ECH12D, **cruising level** 9,800 meters, runway-in-use 28, squawk 6312. **After departure contact Approach on 123.3.**
P: Cleared to Seoul via flight planned route, initial altitude 900 meters on QNH 998, ECH12D, cruising level 9,800 meters, runway-in-use 28, squawk 6312. After departure contact Approach on 123.3, AAR3365.
C: AAR3365, read-back correct.

离场，起始爬升高度修正海压 900 米，修正海压 1 011，航路上申请巡航高度层 9 800 米，应答机 5310，离地后联系进近 123.8。
P： 可以沿计划航路放行至北京，使用跑道 17，PIKAS11D 离场，起始高度修正海压 900 米，修正海压 1 011，航路上申请巡航高度层 9 800 米，应答机 5310，离地后联系进近 123.8，CCA102。
C： CCA102，复诵正确。联系地面 121.65，再见。

P： 大连地面，AAR3365，目的地首尔，通播 G，请求放行许可。
C： AAR3365，通播 G 有效，可以沿计划航路放行至首尔，起始高度修正海压 900 米，修正海压 998，ECH12D 离场，巡航高度层 9 800 米，使用跑道 28，应答机 6312，离地后联系进近 123.3。
P： 可以沿计划航路放行至首尔，起始高度修正海压 900 米，修正海压 998，ECH12D 离场，巡航高度层 9 800 米，使用跑道 28，应答机 6312，离地后联系进近 123.3，AAR3365。
C： AAR3365，复诵正确。

2.5 推出开车

通常情况下，航空器在停放时机头朝向候机楼，在离场时需利用推车将航空器推出停机位，称为 push-back。少数航空器能利用自身动力推出，称为 power-back。根据机场程序，驾驶员可向空管部门或机坪管制部门申请推出。

航空器开车前需要向管制员提出申请，有助于管制员做计划，避免航空器在地面等待时间过长，耗费过多燃油。航空器在提出开车申请时，应表明航空器位置和已接收的通播代号。

2.5.1 单词与词组

push-back	推出
at own discretion	自己决定
slot time	时隙（航空器预计离场时间段）
stand	停机位
gate	登机门，停机位
stand by	稍等
start up	开车（启动发动机）

| breakdown | 故障 |

2.5.2 🔊 听录音

2.5.3 范例

(1) **P:** Dongfang Tower, GIA893, Stand 27, request push-back.
C: GIA893, **push-back approved**.

P：东方塔台，GIA893，27 号位，请求推出。
C：GIA893，同意推出。

(2) **P:** Dongfang Tower, KLM4302, Stand 27, request push-back.
C: KLM4302, stand by. **Expect one minute delay due** B747 taxiing behind.

P：东方塔台，KLM4302，27 号位，请求推出。
C：KLM4302，稍等。由于 B747 在后面滑行，预计延误一分钟。

(3) **P:** Dongfang Tower, QFA129, Gate 24, request start up, Information B.
C: QFA129, **start up approved**.

P：东方塔台，QFA129，24 号桥，请求开车，通播 B。
C：QFA129，同意开车。

(4) **P:** Dongfang Tower, ANZ080, Stand 24, request start up, Information B.
C: ANZ080, **start up at 35**.

P：东方塔台，ANZ080，24 号位，请求开车，通播 B。
C：ANZ080，35 分开车。

(5) **P:** Dongfang Tower, AAR3365, Stand 24, request start up, Information B.
C: AAR3365, expect start up time at 35.

P：东方塔台，AAR3365，24 号位，请求开车，通播 B。
C：AAR3365，预计开车 35 分。

(6) **P:** Dongfang Tower, AFR381, Gate 24, request start up, Information B.
C: AFR381, expect departure 49, **start up at own discretion**.

P：东方塔台，AFR381，24 号桥，请求开车，通播 B。
C：AFR381，预计离场 49 分，开车时间自己掌握。

(7) **C:** CKK206, can you taxi in under your own power or do you want to be towed?

C：CKK206，能靠自身动力滑回来吗？还是需要拖车拖？

2.6 滑出

离场航空器准备就绪，在得到管制员的滑行指令后离开停机位，滑行到起飞跑道外等待点。在一些大型机场，由于拥有多条跑道，以及跑道和滑行道的设计问题，导致航空器在滑行前往跑道的过程中，可能需要穿越另一条跑道。

2.6.1 单词与词组

| taxi | 滑行 |

taxi with caution	滑行时注意
hold	等待
holding point	等待点
backtrack	反向滑行
hold short of	在……外等待
hold position	原地等待
vacate	脱离
cross	穿越
give way to	给……让路
follow	跟在……后面
overtake	超越
expedite	加速
traffic in sight	看到活动
hangar	机库
trench	壕沟

2.6.2 🔊听录音

2.6.3 范例

(1) **P:** Dongfang Tower, LKE1912, Stand 27, request taxi.
C: LKE1912, Dongfang Tower, **taxi to holding point Runway** 18L **via Taxiway** H3, A6 and B, **hold short of** Runway 18L.

P：东方塔台，LKE1912，27 号位，请求滑行。
C：LKE1912，东方塔台，沿滑行道 H3、A6、B 滑到 18 左跑道等待点，在 18 左跑道外等待。

(2) **P:** Dongfang Tower, GDC7128, heavy, Stand 27, request taxi, Information C.
C: GDC7128, Dongfang Tower, taxi to holding point Runway 27, **give way to** B747 passing left to right.

P：东方塔台，GDC7128，重型，27 号位，请求滑行，通播 C。
C：GDC7128，东方塔台，滑到 27 号跑道等待点，给从左向右滑行的 B747 让路。

(3) **P:** Dongfang Tower, DAL185, Stand 36, **request backtrack** at present position.
C: DAL185, Dongfang Tower, **backtrack approved**.

P：东方塔台，DAL185，36 号位，请求从当前位置反向滑行。
C：DAL185，东方塔台，同意反向滑行。

(4) **P:** Dongfang Tower, CES5301, approaching holding point, **request crossing Runway 22**.
C: CES5301, **cross Runway 22**, **report vacated**.
P: CES5301, crossing.
　　(A moment later)
P: CES5301, **runway vacated**.

P：东方塔台，CES5301，接近等待点，请求穿越 22 号跑道。
C：CES5301，穿越 22 号跑道，脱离报告。
P：CES5301，正在穿跑道。
　　（稍后）
P：CES5301，已脱离跑道。

2.7 起飞

当航空器滑行至跑道等待点后，未经管制员允许，应在跑道外等待。管制员下达进入跑道指令后，航空器方可进入跑道。

在得到塔台管制员的起飞许可后，航空器开始起飞。起飞指航空器从起飞线开始滑行到离开地面，爬升到安全高度的加速运动过程。

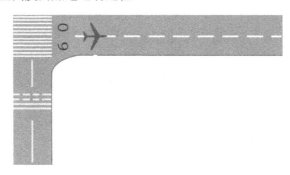

2.7.1 单词与词组

line up	进跑道
airborne	离地，升空
take-off	起飞
departure	离场
climb straight ahead	直线爬升

2.7.2 🔊 听录音

2.7.3 范例

(1) C: DAL185, report ready for departure.
P: Wilco, DAL185.
　　(A moment later)
P: DAL185, ready.
C: DAL185, **Runway 09, line up and wait**.
P: Lining up, Runway 09, DAL185.
C: DAL185, **wind 360 degrees, 4 m/s, Runway 09, cleared for take-off**.
P: Runway 09, cleared for take-off, DAL185.

C：DAL185，准备好报。
P：照办，DAL185。
　　(稍后)
P：DAL185，准备好了。
C：DAL185，进跑道 09 等待。
P：进跑道，跑道 09，DAL185。
C：DAL185，地面风 360 度，4 米每秒，跑道 09，可以起飞。
P：跑道 09，可以起飞，DAL185。

(2) C: AAL186, report the Airbus on final in sight.
P: Airbus in sight, AAL186.
C: AAL186, **after the landing traffic, line up and wait behind**.

C：AAL186，看到五边上的空客报告。
P：看到空客了，AAL186。
C：AAL186，跟在落地飞机后面进跑道等待。

P: After the Airbus line up and wait behind, AAL186.

P: 跟在落地飞机后面进跑道等待，AAL186。

(3) **C:** CDG4670, Dongfang Tower, Runway 18, cleared for take-off.
P: Cleared for take-off, Runway 18, CDG4670.
　　(A moment later)
C: CDG4670, **take off immediately or vacate runway**①.

C: CDG4670，东方塔台，跑道 18，可以起飞。
P: 可以起飞，跑道 18，CDG4670。
　　（稍后）
C: CDG4670，立即起飞，否则脱离跑道。

(4) **C:** CPA347, **take off immediately or hold short of runway**.
P: Holding short, CPA347.

C: CPA347，立即起飞，否则在跑道外等待。
P: 跑道外等待，CPA347。

(5) **C:** EVA712, Dongfang Tower, Runway 18, cleared for take-off.
P: Cleared for take-off, Runway 18, EVA712.
　　(A moment later)
C: EVA712, **hold position, cancel take-off, I say again, cancel take-off**②.
P: Holding, EVA712.

C: EVA712，东方塔台，跑道 18，可以起飞。
P: 可以起飞，跑道 18，EVA712。
　　（稍后）
C: EVA712，原地等待，取消起飞指令，再说一遍，取消起飞指令。
P: 等待，EVA712。

(6) **C:** UAE309, Dongfang Tower, Runway 18, cleared for take-off.
P: Cleared for take-off, Runway 18, UAE309.
　　(UAE309 starts take-off roll.)
C: UAE309, **stop immediately**, UAE309, **stop immediately**.
P: Stopping, UAE309.

C: UAE309，东方塔台，跑道 18，可以起飞。
P: 可以起飞，跑道 18，UAE309。
　　（UAE309 开始起飞滑跑。）
C: UAE309，立即停止起飞，UAE309，立即停止起飞。
P: 中断起飞，UAE309。

---

① 当起飞许可未被执行时。
② 航空器处于静止状态时取消起飞许可。

第 3 章 进近管制——离场阶段

航空器起飞后,塔台管制员将其移交给进近管制员指挥。在非常繁忙的终端管制区,进近管制可划分为不同的管制席位,各自承担不同的管制职责,如离场雷达管制、进场雷达管制和五边雷达管制等。在提供空中交通监视(雷达)服务时,管制员应使用一般雷达管制用语、二次监视雷达用语和进近雷达管制用语等雷达管制标准术语。

对于 IFR 离场的航空器而言,管制员的指令主要涉及高度的改变和路径的选择两方面。高度的改变以上升指令为主,高度保持指令为辅;而路径的选择则以指定离场程序(标准仪表离场程序或 RNAV 离场程序)或具体航向、航迹的方式体现。除了常规指令以外,当航空器之间存在飞行冲突或其他必要情况时,通常要进行活动通报。

通过本章的学习,应达到以下学习目标:

- ❖ 掌握雷达管制基本用语;
- ❖ 掌握 IFR 航空器离场的用语;
- ❖ 掌握飞行活动通报的相关用语;
- ❖ 理解飞行活动冲突通报的时机及内容。

3.1 雷达管制用语

一般雷达管制用语既可用于一次监视雷达设备也可用于二次监视雷达设备提供的管制服务中,而二次监视雷达用语只适用于航空器配备机载应答机的二次监视雷达管制服务中。进近雷达管制用语是进近管制员指挥航空器进场和进近时的用语。本节主要介绍一般雷达管制用语和二次监视雷达用语。进近雷达管制用语将在第 5 章进行介绍。

3.1.1 单词与词组

identification	识别
radar contact	雷达看到
identified	已经识别
resume own navigation	恢复自主领航
direct	直飞
magnetic track	磁航迹
remain this frequency	保持长守
terminate	终止
orbit	盘旋
transponder	应答机
radio contact lost	失去无线电联络
observed	看到了

if you read	如果你能听到
low altitude warning	低高度告警
minimum flight altitude	最低飞行高度
terrain alert	近地告警

3.1.2 🔊 听录音

3.1.3 范例

(1) **C:** THY021, **report heading and level**.
　　P: Heading 140, maintaining 3,000 meters, THY021.
　　C: THY021, **for identification, turn left heading 110**.
　　P: Left heading 110, THY021.
　　　(A moment later)
　　P: Wuhan Approach, THY021, on heading 110.
　　C: THY021, **identified, position 20 kilometers north of CON, continue present heading.**
　　P: Continue present heading, THY021.

　　C：THY021，报告航向高度。
　　P：航向140，高度3 000米保持，THY021。
　　C：THY021，为了识别，左转航向110。
　　P：左转航向110，THY021。
　　　（稍后）
　　P：武汉进近，THY021，航向110。
　　C：THY021，已经识别，位置从化以北20公里，保持现在航向。
　　P：保持现在航向，THY021。

(2) **C:** DLH723, **not identified**. Not yet within radar coverage. **Resume own navigation, direct CHG, magnetic track 200, distance 32 kilometers.**
　　P: Resume own navigation, direct CHG, DLH723.

　　C：DLH723，没有识别。还未到雷达覆盖范围内，恢复自主领航，直飞朝阳，磁航迹200，距离32公里。
　　P：恢复自主领航，直飞朝阳，DLH723。

(3) **C:** CSZ9783, **identification lost due radar failure.** Contact Dongfang Control on 126.25.
　　P: 126.25, CSZ9783.

　　C：CSZ9783，由于雷达失效，识别丢失，联系东方区域126.25。
　　P：126.25，CSZ9783。

(4) **C:** CCA3653, **will shortly lose identification due blind area. Remain this frequency.**
　　P: Wilco, CCA3653.

　　C：CCA3653，由于雷达盲区，将短时失去雷达识别，保持长守。
　　P：照办，CCA3653。

(5) **C:** HBH8380, **turn right heading 350 for spacing**.
　　P: Right heading 350, HBH8380.
　　C: HBH8380, **stop turn, heading 290**.
　　P: Heading 290, HBH8380.

　　C：HBH8380，因为间隔，右转航向350。
　　P：右转航向350，HBH8380。
　　C：HBH8380，停止转弯，航向290。
　　P：航向290，HBH8380。

(6) C: CSC8861, **after HO, fly heading 010**.
P: After HO, fly heading 010, CSC8861.

C：CSC8861，过长武后，航向飞 010。
P：过长武后，航向飞 010，CSC8861。

(7) C: CSN9586, report heading.
P: Heading 240, CSN9586.
C: CSN9586, **continue heading 240**.
P: Continue heading 240, CSN9586.

C：CSN9586，报告航向。
P：航向 240，CSN9586。
C：CSN9586，保持航向 240。
P：保持航向 240，CSN9586。

(8) C: CHH345, **make a three sixty turn left for sequencing**.
P: Three sixty turn left, CHH345.

C：CHH345，因为排序，左转三百六十度①。
P：左转三百六十度，CHH345。

(9) C: CXA8470, **orbit left for delay**.
P: Orbit left, CXA8470

C：CXA8470，因为延迟，左转盘旋。
P：左转盘旋，CXA8470。

(10) C: ACA050, **resume own navigation to DAL**②, position 15 kilometers north of DAL.
P: Direct DAL, resume own navigation, ACA050.

C：ACA050，恢复自主领航，飞往大理，位置大理以北 15 公里。
P：飞往大理，恢复自主领航，ACA050。

(11) C: GCR7896, **position 12 kilometers from touchdown, radar service terminated**, contact Tower 118.1.
P: 118.1, GCR7896.

C：GCR7896，位置距接地点 12 公里，雷达服务终止，联系塔台 118.1。
P：118.1，GCR7896。

(12) C: UAL326, **advise transponder capability**.
P: Transponder Charlie, UAL326.
C: UAL326, **squawk** 6411.
P: 6411, UAL326.
C: UAL326, **confirm squawk**.
P: Squawking 6411, UAL326.
C: UAL326, **reset** squawk 6411.
P: Resetting 6411, UAL326.
C: UAL326, radar contact. Climb to 4,500 meters.
P: Climbing to 4,500 meters, UAL326.

C：UAL326，报告应答机能力。
P：模式 C 应答机，UAL326。
C：UAL326，应答机 6411。
P：6411，UAL326。
C：UAL326，证实应答机。
P：应答机 6411，UAL326。
C：UAL326，重新设定应答机 6411。
P：重新设定应答机 6411，UAL326。
C：UAL326，雷达看到，上升到 4 500 米。
P：上升到 4 500 米，UAL326。

(13) C: JAL345, **check altimeter setting and confirm level**.
P: Altimeter 1,003, 3,600 meters, JAL345.
C: JAL345, **stop squawk Charlie, wrong indication**.

C：JAL345，检查高度表设定值，证实高度。
P：修正海压 1 003，高度 3 600 米，JAL345。
C：JAL345，关闭应答机 C 模式，指示错误。

---

① 实际工作中管制员多用"左转盘旋一圈"来表达。
② 此处来自 ICAO 2007 版 9432 号文件 *Manual of Radiotelephony*。

(14) C: B3475, **radio contact lost. If you read, squawk IDENT, I say again, squawk IDENT**.

(A moment later)

C: B3475, **squawk observed, will continue radar control, squawk IDENT to acknowledge**.

C：B3475，失去无线电联络，如果你能听到，应答机识别，我重复一遍，应答机识别。

（稍后）

C：B3475，应答机识别看到了，将继续雷达管制，应答机识别进行认收。

(15) C: CHB6237, **reply not received**. If you read, turn left heading 150, I say again, turn left heading 150.

(A moment later)

C: CHB6237, **turn observed**, position 15 kilometers south of VYK VOR, will continue radar control.

C：CHB6237，回答没有收到，如果你能听到，左转航向 150，我重复一遍，左转航向 150。

（稍后）

C：CHB6237，转弯看到了，位置大王庄以南 15 公里，将继续雷达管制。

(16) C: TBA9907, **low altitude warning**, check your altitude immediately, QNH 1,006, minimum flight altitude 650 meters.

P: Roger, TBA9907.

C：TBA9907，低高度告警，立即检查高度，修正海压 1 006，最低飞行高度 650 米。

P：收到，TBA9907。

(17) C: CSN6580, **terrain alert**, climb to 900 meters, QNH 1,006.

P: Climbing to 900 meters, QNH 1,006, CSN6580.

C：CSN6580，近地告警，上升到修正海压 900 米，修正海压 1 006。

P：上升到修正海压 900 米，修正海压 1 006，CSN6580。

3.2 离场指令

一般来说，空中交通监视服务中航空器的离场方式主要由驾驶员自主领航离场（标准仪表离场程序和 RNAV 离场程序）、雷达引导离场和组合离场三种组成。管制员根据需要，向离场航空器发布相应的指令。

3.2.1 单词与词组

airborne	离地
present heading	现在航向
runway heading	跑道航向
report	报告
report reaching/passing	到达/通过报告
correction	更正
on track	在航迹上
expedite	加速
conflicting traffic	冲突活动
MET report	气象报告
abeam	正切

3.2.2 🔊 听录音

3.2.3 范例

(1) **P:** Dongfang Departure, CCA1352, **airborne**, Runway 18, **passing 300 meters climbing to 900 meters**, with you.

C: CCA1352, Dongfang Departure, **radar contact**, **follow BAV 01 Departure**, continue climb to 2,700 meters on QNH 998.

P: BAV 01 Departure, climbing to 2,700 meters on QNH 998, CCA1352.

(A moment later)

C: CCA1352, continue climb to 5,400 meters on standard.

P: Continue climb to 5,400 meters, CCA1352.

(A moment later)

P: CCA1352, 5,400 meters maintaining.

C: CCA1352, contact Dongfang Control on 120.1, good day.

P: 120.1 for Control, CCA1352, good day.

(2) **P:** Dongfang Departure, CDG1835, heavy.

C: CDG1835, Dongfang Departure, identified, **cancel SID, continue runway heading**, climb to 3,600 meters, **after passing 3,000 meters, proceed direct to P40**.

P: Continue runway heading 040, climb to 3,600 meters, after passing 3,000 meters, direct P40, CDG1835.

C: CDG1835, report passing 3,000 meters.
P: Wilco, CDG1835.
(A moment later)
P: CDG1835, passing 3,000 meters, estimating P40 1324.
C: CDG1835, roger.
C: CDG1835, contact Dongfang Control 127.3, good day.
P: 127.3, CDG1835.

(3) **P:** Dongfang Departure, DAL185, airborne, Runway 23R, with you.

P: 东方离场,CCA1352,离地,跑道18,通过300米上升到900米,听你指挥了。
C: CCA1352,东方离场,雷达看到,包头01号离场,继续上升到修正海压2 700米,修正海压998。
P: 包头01号离场,上升到修正海压2 700米,修正海压998,CCA1352。
(稍后)
C: CCA1352,继续上升到标准气压5 400米。
P: 继续上升到5 400米,CCA1352。
(稍后)
P: CCA1352,5 400米保持。
C: CCA1352,联系东方区域120.1,再见。
P: 区域120.1,CCA1352,再见。

P: 东方离场,CDG1835,重型。
C: CDG1835,东方离场,已经识别,取消标准离场,保持跑道航向,上升到3 600米,通过3 000米以后,直飞P40。
P: 保持跑道航向040,上升到3 600米,通过3 000米以后,直飞P40,CDG1835。
C: CDG1835,通过3 000米报告。
P: 照办,CDG1835。
(稍后)
P: CDG1835,通过3 000米,预计P40 1324。
C: CDG1835,收到。
C: CDG1835,联系东方区域127.3,再见。
P: 127.3,CDG1835。

P: 东方离场,DAL185,离地,跑道23右,听你指挥了。

C: DAL185, Dongfang Departure, radar contact, follow VYK 01 departure, climb to and maintain 1,500 meters on QNH 1,003.

P: VYK 01 Departure, climbing to 1,500 meters, QNH 1,003, DAL185.

C: DAL185, cancel SID, turn right heading 050 due traffic.

P: Cancel SID, turn right heading 050, DAL185.

P: Dongfang Departure, DAL185, on heading 050.

C: DAL185, roger, climb to and maintain 6,600 meters on standard.

P: Climbing to 6,600 meters on standard, DAL185.

C: DAL185, turn left direct to RENOB, resume own navigation, **magnetic track 320, distance 15 kilometers**.

P: Turn left direct RENOB, resume own navigation, DAL185.

C: DAL185, contact Dongfang Control on 125.65.
P: Contact Dongfang Control on 125.65, DAL185.

(4) P: Beijing Departure, HDA396, airborne, Runway 36L, climbing to 900 meters.

C: HDA396, Beijing Departure, **confirm squawking** 4523.

P: Affirm, HDA396.

C: HDA396, radar contact, **follow CHEDY ONE RNAV Departure, cross AA018 waypoint at or above 3,600 meters**, climb to and maintain 5,400 meters.

P: Climbing to 5,400 meters, CHEDY ONE RNAV Departure, cross AA018 at 3,600 meters or above, HDA396.

C: HDA396, contact Beijing Control on 128.5.
P: Control on 128.5, HDA396.

(5) C: CPA589, turn right heading 150, vectoring for spacing, maintain 2,700 meters, **expect to resume LADIX ONE RNAV Departure**.

P: Right heading 150, maintaining 2,700 meters, expecting LADIX ONE RNAV Departure, CPA589.

C: DAL185，东方离场，雷达看到，大王庄 01 号离场，上升到修正海压 1 500 米保持，修正海压 1 003。

P: 大王庄 01 号离场，上升到修正海压 1 500 米，修正海压 1 003，DAL185。

C: DAL185，取消标准离场，右转航向 050，因为活动。

P: 取消标准离场，右转航向 050，DAL185。

P: 东方离场，DAL185，航向 050。

C: DAL185，收到。上升到标准气压 6 600 米保持。

P: 上升到标准气压 6 600 米，DAL185。

C: DAL185，左转直飞 RENOB，恢复自主领航，磁航迹 320，距离 15 公里。

P: 左转直飞 RENOB，恢复自主领航，DAL185。

C: DAL185，联系东方区域 125.65。
P: 联系东方区域 125.65，DAL185。

P: 北京离场，HDA396，离地，跑道 36 左，上升到 900 米。

C: HDA396，北京离场，证实应答机 4523。

P: 是的，HDA396。

C: HDA396，雷达看到，按照 CHEDY 1 RNAV 离场，过 AA018 高度不低于 3 600 米，上升到 5 400 米保持。

P: 上升到 5 400 米，CHEDY 1 RNAV 离场，过 AA018 高度不低于 3 600 米，HDA396。

C: HDA396，联系北京区域 128.5。
P: 区域 128.5，HDA396。

C: CPA589，由于间隔，雷达引导右转航向 150，保持 2 700 米，预计将恢复到 LADIX 1 RNAV 离场。

P: 右转航向 150，保持 2 700 米，预计 LADIX 1 RNAV 离场，CPA589。

(6) **C: AAL126, fly heading 260, resume LADIX ONE RNAV Departure.**

P: Heading 260, resume LADIX ONE RNAV Departure, AAL126.

(7) **C: DLH457, cleared direct AA011, resume LADIX ONE RNAV Departure, comply with restrictions.**

P: Direct AA011, resume LADIX ONE RNAV Departure, comply with restrictions, DLH457.

(8) C1: B3475, you are now clear of controlled airspace. Contact Dongfang Information on 129.9.

P: Dongfang on 129.9, B3475.

（A moment later）

P: Dongfang Information, B3475, MA60, departed from Nanyuan Airport 1400, direct to Taiyuan Airport, VMC, climbing from 1,800 meters to 3,000 meters. Request any known conflicting traffic information.

C2: B3475, Dongfang Information, no reported traffic.

C：AAL126，航向飞 260，恢复 LADIX 1 RNAV 离场。

P：航向 260，恢复 LADIX 1 RNAV 离场，AAL126。

C：DLH457，可以直飞 AA011，恢复 LADIX 1 RNAV 离场，按程序限制执行。

P：直飞 AA011，恢复 LADIX 1 RNAV 离场，按程序限制执行，DLH457。

C1：B3475，正在离开管制空域，联系东方情报 129.9。

P：东方 129.9，B3475。

（稍后）

P：东方情报，B3475，新舟 60，1400 分从南苑机场起飞，直飞太原机场，目视气象条件，从 1 800 米上升到 3 000 米，请求飞行活动情报。

C2：B3475，东方情报，没有活动报告。

3.3 飞行活动通报

飞行活动通报是陆空通话中一项重要的内容。当航空器之间存在飞行冲突，或在其他一些必要的情况下，管制员通常需要给相关的航空器发送活动通报，让驾驶员保持必要的情景意识，增加更多的安全保护。

飞行活动通报术语与标准的管制指令略有不同，它具有简练性、灵活性、多样性等特点。其核心内容是信息，而不是操作指令，管制员通常需要根据即时的空中交通态势迅速选择通报的内容，做到精练且实用。

3.3.1 单词与词组

unknown	不明飞行
opposite direction	相对飞行
same direction	同向飞行
11 o'clock	11 点钟方位
crossing left to right	从左向右穿越
negative contact	没有看到
vectors	引导
fast moving	快速移动
closing	接近

converging	汇聚
diverging	分散
parallel	平行飞行
overtaking	超越

3.3.2 🔊 听录音

3.3.3 典型格式与范例

> 飞行活动情报通常包括方位、飞行方向、距离、机型、高度等，可以如下形式给出：
> （1）以 12 小时制时钟形式表示冲突活动的相对方位；
> （2）使用公里（海里）表示与冲突航空器的距离；
> （3）冲突航空器的预计飞行方向；
> （4）航空器的高度和机型（如果不明，可描述冲突航空器的相对速度，如慢或快）。
> 具体格式如下：
> TRAFFIC (number) O'CLOCK (distance) (direction of flight) [any pertinent information].

范例：

(1) C: AFR565, **unknown traffic, 1 o'clock, 15 kilometers, opposite direction, fast moving, report traffic in sight**.
P: **Looking out**, AFR565.
　(A moment later)
P: AFR565, traffic in sight.

C：AFR565，不明飞行活动，1 点钟方位，15 公里，相对飞行，快速移动，看到活动报告。
P：正在观察，AFR565。
　（稍后）
P：AFR565，看到活动。

(2) C: CSC215, unknown traffic, 10 o'clock, 11 **miles, crossing left to right**, fast moving, report traffic in sight.
P: CSC215, negative contact, request vectors.
C: CSC215, turn left heading 050.
P: Turning left heading 050, CSC215.
C: CSC215, **clear of traffic**, resume own navigation, direct P23.
P: Direct P23, CSC215.

C：CSC215，不明飞行活动，10 点钟方位，11 海里，从左向右穿越，快速移动，看到活动报告。
P：CSC215，没有看到，请求引导。
C：CSC215，左转航向 050。
P：左转航向 050，CSC215。
C：CSC215，没有影响，恢复自主领航，直飞 P23。
P：直飞 P23，CSC215。

(3) C: CHH7873, traffic, 10 o'clock, 12 kilometers, **northbound**, MA60, **above you**.
P: Looking out, CHH7873.
C: CHH7873, **do you want vectors**?
P: Negative vectors, traffic in sight, CHH7873.

C：CHH7873，飞行活动通报，10 点钟方位，12 公里，向北飞行，新舟 60，高于你。
P：正在观察，CHH7873。
C：CHH7873，需要引导吗？
P：不需要引导，看到活动，CHH7873。

(4) **C:** AMU866, traffic at 10 o'clock, 8 kilometers, **closing from left, indicating slightly below**, fast moving.

C：AMU866，飞行活动通报，10 点钟方位，8 公里，从左侧接近，高度略低于你，快速移动。

(5) **C:** CSN3369, **turn right 30 degrees immediately to avoid traffic at** 11 o'clock, 5 kilometers.
P: Turning right 30 degrees, CSN3369.
C: CSN3369, clear of traffic, resume own navigation, direct NCH.
P: Resume own navigation, direct NCH, CSN3369.

C：CSN3369，立即右转 30 度避让 11 点钟方位 5 公里的活动。
P：右转 30 度，CSN3369。
C：CSN3369，没有影响，恢复自主领航，直飞昌北。
P：恢复自主领航，直飞昌北，CSN3369。

(6) **C:** CPA102, Beijing Approach, turn left immediately **heading 330 to avoid unknown traffic**, 12 o'clock, 10 kilometers, fast moving.
P: Turning left heading 330, CPA102.

C：CPA102，北京进近，立刻左转航向 330，避让不明飞行活动，12 点钟方位，10 公里，快速移动。
P：左转航向 330，CPA102。

(7) **C:** CSN3978, Xi'an Approach, **traffic is unmanned free balloon**, estimated over NSH **at** 19, **level unknown**, **moving** west.
P: Roger, traffic in sight, CSN3978.

C：CSN3978，西安进近，无人驾驶自由气球，预计过宁陕 19 分，高度不明，向西方移动。
P：收到，看到活动，CSN3978。

第4章 区域管制

区域管制管辖空间大，航空器飞行时间长，管制员使用的通话用语相对更加丰富。除了一般的高度、速度和航向指令以外，还要涉及与航路等待、缩小垂直间隔（RVSM）、侧向偏置（SLOP）、绕飞雷雨等相关的通话用语。

通过本章的学习，应达到以下学习目标：

- ❖ 掌握高度指令的发布；
- ❖ 掌握管制员要求驾驶员的额外位置报告，以及向航空器提供位置信息的方式和内容；
- ❖ 掌握等待指令的发布；
- ❖ 理解RVSM运行的指令；
- ❖ 理解驾驶员位置报告的内容；
- ❖ 了解绕飞雷雨的常用指令；
- ❖ 了解航空器加入、穿越或离开航路的指令。

4.1 高度信息

离场（或进近）管制员在航空器达到一定高度后，将其移交给区域管制员。区域管制员指挥航空器继续上升至巡航高度。进入巡航阶段后，因为颠簸、结冰等原因，航空器可能会申请调整高度，管制员在考虑整体交通后做出决定。某些时候，由于载荷限制，航空器可能无法执行管制员的高度指令。当航空器接近目的地时，航空器需要下降高度以实施进近着陆。

需要注意的是，在不同的飞行阶段及高度表设定基准下，高度可以是海拔高度（altitude）、高（height）或者飞行高度层（flight level）。

4.1.1 单词与词组

report	报告
reach	到达
available	可用
unavailable	不可用
further climb	继续上升
heavy traffic	交通繁忙
congested	堵塞的，拥挤的
leave	离开
rate of descent	下降率
rate of climb	上升率

	maintain	保持
	odd levels	单数高度层
	even levels	双数高度层

4.1.2 🔊 听录音

4.1.3 范例

(1) **C:** AAL138, **report** level.
P: Maintaining 3,000 meters, AAL138.

C：AAL138，报告高度。
P：保持 3 000 米，AAL138。

(2) **C:** AIC349, **report leaving/reaching/passing** 7,500 meters.
P: Wilco, AIC349.
　　(A moment later)
P: AIC349, leaving /reaching/passing 7,500 meters.

C：AIC349，离开/到达/通过 7 500 米报告。
P：照办，AIC349。
（稍后）
P：AIC349，离开/到达/通过 7 500 米。

(3) **C:** CBJ5154, maintain 8,100 meters **until further advised**.
P: Maintaining 8,100 meters, CBJ5154.

C：CBJ5154，在进一步通知前，保持 8 100 米。
P：保持 8 100 米，CBJ5154。

(4) **C:** AAR3213, climb to 7,500 meters.
P: Leaving 6,300 meters, climbing to 7,500 meters, AAR3213.

C：AAR3213，上升到 7 500 米。
P：离开 6 300 米，上升到 7 500 米，AAR3213。

(5) **C:** CCA1709, Dongfang Approach, after passing RENOB, descend to 4,500 meters.
P: After RENOB, descend to 4,500 meters, CCA1709.

C：CCA1709，东方进近，通过 RENOB 后，下降到 4 500 米。
P：RENOB 后，下降到 4 500 米，CCA1709。

(6) **C:** CXA8586, **stop descent at** 5,100 meters.
P: Stopping descent at 5,100 meters, CXA8586.

C：CXA8586，在 5 100 米停止下降。
P：5 100 米停止下降，CXA8586。

(7) **C:** CES5173, **continue climb to** 10,100 meters.
P: Climbing to 10,100 meters, CES5173.

C：CES5173，继续上升到 10 100 米。
P：上升到 10 100 米，CES5173。

(8) **C:** DLH7323, recleared 9,500 meters.
P: Recleared 9,500 meters, DLH7323.

C：DLH7323，重新许可到 9 500 米。
P：重新许可到 9 500 米，DLH7323。

(9) **C:** HDA901, climb to 10,400 meters, **expedite until passing** 9,200 meters.

C：HDA901，上升到 10 400 米，尽快通过 9 200 米。

P: Climbing to 10,400 meters, expediting until passing 9,200 meters, HDA901.
　　(or)
P: Unable to expedite due weight, HDA901.

P：上升到10 400米，尽快加速通过9 200米，HDA901。
　　（或）
P：由于超重，不能加速，HDA901。

(10) C: CSN3201, Beijing Control, **climb at** 10 m/s.

C：CSN3201，北京区域，上升率10米每秒。

(11) C: CES2020, Beijing Control, climb at 2,000 ft/min **or greater**.

C：CES2020，北京区域，上升率不小于2 000英尺每分钟。

(12) C: AHK8783, Shanghai Control, climb at 1,500 ft/min **or less**.

C：AHK8783，上海区域，上升率不大于1 500英尺每分钟。

(13) C: CKK206, Beijing Control, **climb to reach** 9,500 meters **by** VYK.

C：CKK206，北京区域，在大王庄前上升到9 500米。

(14) C: GCR6529, Beijing Control, **descend to reach** 7,200 meters **at** 05.

C：GCR6529，北京区域，在05分下降到7 200米。

(15) C: CHH7988, Beijing Control, **advise if able to cross** HUR at 6,300 meters.
P: Affirm, CHH7988.
C: CHH7988, **climb to and maintain** 6,300 meters.

C：CHH7988，北京区域，如果能在6 300米通过怀柔，请通知我。
P：是的，CHH7988。
C：CHH7988，上升到6 300米保持。

(16) C: CSC8825, Beijing Control, **when ready, climb to** 10,100 meters.

C：CSC8825，北京区域，准备好后，上升到10 100米。

(17) C: ANA917, can you reach 10,100 meters by VYK?

C：ANA917，能在大王庄之前到达10 100米吗？

(18) C: CAL503, 9,500 meters is **not available** due to heavy traffic. **Can you accept** 11,300 meters?

C：CAL503，9 500米已经被占用，飞机较多。你能接受11 300米吗？

(19) P: CPA6111, TCAS RA.
C: CPA6111, roger, **report returning to clearance**.
　　(A moment later)
P: CPA6111, clear of conflict, returning to clearance. Now maintaining 7,500 meters.
C: Dongang Control, roger.

P：CPA6111，TCAS RA告警。
C：CPA6111，收到，返回许可高度报告。
　　（稍后）
P：CPA6111，冲突解除，正在返回许可高度，保持7 500米。
C：东方区域，收到。

4.2 位置信息

航空器飞越强制性报告点时，按照规定，需要进行位置报告，除非管制员要求其省略位置报告（雷达管制时）。管制员如果觉得必要，也可以要求航空器进行额外的位置报告。无论如何，在航空器离开管制范围之前，都需要让其恢复正常的位置报告。

雷达管制环境下，管制员有时需要为航空器提供位置信息，以帮助驾驶员准确掌握自己的位置。

4.2.1 单词与词组

omit position reports	省略位置报告
intercept	截获
pass	通过
radial	径向线
resume position reporting	恢复位置报告
over	上空
abeam	正切

4.2.2 🔊 听录音

4.2.3 典型格式及范例

---
1. 驾驶员进行位置报告的格式

（1）航空器呼号；
（2）报告点名称；
（3）过报告点时间；
（4）当前高度；
（5）下一报告点名称；
（6）预计过报告点时间；
（7）再下一个报告点名称。

范例 1：

(1) **P:** Beijing Control, CCA1212, **over** YQG, **at** 15, maintaining 8,400 meters, **estimating** BTO at 35, next VYK .

P：北京区域，CCA1212，遥墙上方，15 分，保持 8 400 米，预计泊头 35 分，下一个点大王庄。

(2) **P:** Beijing Control, CSN6723, over BTO, at 35, maintaining 8,400 meters, estimating VYK at 50.

P：北京区域，CSN6723，泊头上方，35 分，保持 8 400 米，预计大王庄 50 分。

(3) **C:** CXA866, Wuhan Control, next report at LKO.

C：CXA866，武汉区域，下一次在龙口报告。

(4) **C:** CKK210, **omit position reports until over** JR.

C：CKK210，省略位置报告直至过良乡。

(5) C: CAL503, **resume position reporting**.   C：CAL503，恢复位置报告。

(6) C: CHH7896, report passing WXI.   C：CHH7896，过魏县报告。

(7) C: GCR6500, report 30 kilometers from HYN DME.   C：GCR6500，距花垣 DME 30 公里报告。

(8) C: ANA917, report passing 320 radial LJG VOR.   C：ANA917，通过连江 VOR 320 径向线报告。

(9) C: CES5321, report distance from NJL DME.
P: 40 kilometers from NJL DME, CES5321.   C：CES5321，报告距禄口 DME 的距离。
P：距禄口 DME 40 公里，CES5321。

---

2. 管制员向驾驶员通报航空器位置的方式

（1）相对于一个大众所知的地理位置；
（2）相对于一个重要点、航路导航台或进近设施的磁航迹与距离；
（3）相对一个大众所知位置的方位与距离；
（4）最后进近时相对于接地端的距离；
（5）相对于 ATS 航路中心线的距离与方位。

范例 2：

(1) C: CCA1901, **position over** HO.   C：CCA1901，位置长武上空。

(2) C: BAW297, resume own navigation, direct DKO, **magnetic track** 073, **distance** 37 kilometers.   C：BAW297，恢复自主领航，直飞磴口，磁航迹 073，距离 37 公里。

(3) C: CXA8459, position 25 kilometers southwest of the field.   C：CXA8459，位置距机场西南 25 公里。

(4) C: CAL2811, **position** 20 kilometers **from touchdown**.   C：CAL2811，位置距接地点 20 公里。

(5) C: AMU127, position 10 kilometers left of the route.   C：AMU127，位置距航路左侧 10 公里。

4.3 航路等待

由于天气变化、飞行冲突或非常规情况等的发生，管制员可能需要指挥航空器在航路上等待，加入标准等待程序。某些情况下，管制员也可以发布 orbit left/right 等指令，以 360 度转弯的机动方式延长航空器的运行时间。当管制员发送等待指令时，一般应告知原因。

4.3.1 单词与词组

hold	等待
right hand circuit	右航线
left hand pattern	左航线
inbound	向台
outbound	背台
deteriorate	恶化
thunderstorm	雷暴
congestion	拥堵
VIP flight	要客
orbit	盘旋

4.3.2 听录音

4.3.3 范例

(1) C: ACA087, **cleared to** WTM, descend to 8,100 meters, **hold as published**, expect approach clearance at 13.
P: Descending to 8,100 meters, hold at WTM, ACA087.

C：ACA087，可以飞往 WTM 等待，下降到 8 100 米，按公布程序等待，预计进近许可时间 13 分。
P：下降到 8 100 米，在 WTM 等待，ACA087。

(2) P: Dongfang Control, BAW038, request detailed holding instructions.
C: BAW038, **proceed to** TOL, maintain 7,200 meters, **hold inbound track** 038 degrees, **left hand pattern**, **outbound time** one and a half minutes, **expect further clearance at** 19.

P：东方区域，BAW038，请求详细等待指令。
C：BAW038，可以飞往 TOL 等待，保持 7 200 米，向台航迹 038 度，左航线，背台一分半钟，预计进一步许可时间 19 分①。

(3) P: Dongfang Control, AFR182, request detailed holding instructions.
C: AFR182, cleared to the 120 radial of the SGM VOR at 30 kilometers DME Fix. Maintain 6,900 meters, **hold east, right hand circuit**, outbound time one and a half minutes, expect further clearance at 36, the holding speed at or below 550 km/h.

P：东方区域，AFR182，请求详细等待指令。
C：AFR182，可以飞往 SGM VOR 120 度径向线 30 公里 DME 定位点等待。保持 6 900 米，在东面等待，右航线，背台一分半钟，预计进一步许可时间 36 分，等待速度不大于 550 公里每小时。

---

① 等待指令内容的发送次序为：等待点+等待高度+向台航迹+左（右）转+背台时间。

(4) P: Dongfang Control, CSN2182, request detailed holding instructions.
C: CSN2182, cleared to the 120 radial of the XSH VOR at 30 kilometers DME Fix. Maintain 6,900 meters, hold between 25 and 35 kilometers DME, right hand circuit, expect approach clearance at 36.

P：东方区域，CSN2182，请求详细等待指令。
C：CSN2182，可以飞往 XSH VOR 120 度径向线 30 公里 DME 定位点。保持 6 900 米，在距 DME 25 到 35 公里之间等待，右航线，预计进近许可时间 36 分。

4.4 RVSM 运行与 SLOP

缩小垂直间隔（RVSM）是相对于常规垂直间隔（conventional vertical separation minima, CVSM）而言的。RVSM 空域在我国指的是飞行高度层为 8 900 米（含）至 12 500 米（含）之间的空域。

策略横向偏置程序（SLOP）允许具备横向偏置能力且符合相关要求的航空器在 RVSM 空域内沿航路（航线）飞行时，向航路中心线（航线）右侧平行偏置一定距离。在 SLOP 通话术语中，"偏置（proceed offset）"是关键词汇。

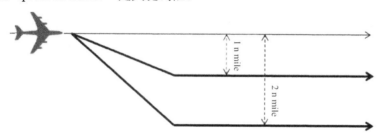

4.4.1 单词与词组

RVSM	缩小垂直间隔标准
offset	偏置
issue	发布
state aircraft	国家航空器①
turbulence	颠簸
resume	恢复

4.4.2 🔊听录音

4.4.3 范例

1. RVSM

(1) C: G-KSIX, Dongfang Control, **confirm**

C：G-KSIX，东方区域，证实是否获

---

① 根据《国际民航公约》规定，用于军事、海关和警察部门的航空器属于国家航空器。

	RVSM approved. P: Dongfang Control, G-KSIX, negative RVSM.	准 RVSM 运行。 P：东方区域，G-KSIX，不是 RVSM。
(2)	P: Dongfang Control, P-ZRVI, **affirm RVSM**.	P：东方区域，P-ZRVI，是 RVSM。
(3)	P: Dongfang Control, G-FPHZ, **negative RVSM, state aircraft**.	P：东方区域，G-FPHZ，不是 RVSM，国家航空器。
(4)	C: F-BCDE, **unable issue clearance into RVSM airspace**, maintain 8,400 meters.	C：F-BCDE，不能发布进入 RVSM 空域的管制许可，保持 8 400 米。
(5)	P: Dongfang Control, P-ZRVI, **unable RVSM due turbulence**.	P：东方区域，P-ZRVI，由于颠簸，不能保持 RVSM。
(6)	P: Dongfang Control, D-BVIQ, **unable RVSM due equipment**.	P：东方区域，D-BVIQ，由于设备原因，不能保持 RVSM。
(7)	C: ZK-NFO, **report when able to resume RVSM**.	C：ZK-NFO，能够恢复 RVSM 时报告。

2. SLOP

(1)	C: G-BCKL, **advise if able to proceed parallel offset**.	C：G-BCKL，请告知能否按照平行偏置飞行。
(2)	C: AFR116, after EPGAM, **proceed offset** 2 miles right of A593.	C：AFR116，EPGAM 后，向 A593 航路中心线右偏置 2 海里。
(3)	C: ANA1260, **cancel offset**, back to A593.	C：ANA1260，取消偏置，回到 A593 航路。
(4)	C: CCA1061, **cancel offset**, proceed direct to GLN.	C：CCA1061，取消偏置，直飞观澜。

4.5 绕飞雷雨

空中遇有雷雨时，情况允许条件下，驾驶员通常采取绕飞的措施。在确认雷雨不再对航空器安全产生影响的情况下，管制员可指挥航空器回到航路。

4.5.1 单词与词组

detour	绕飞
go round	绕飞
circumnavigate	绕飞
deviate	偏离
CB (cumulonimbus)	积雨云

build-up	积雨云
adverse weather	恶劣天气
hazardous weather	恶劣天气
severe weather	恶劣天气
turbulence	颠簸
icing	积冰
anti-icing	防冰
de-icing	除冰
thunderstorm	雷暴
clear air turbulence (CAT)	晴空颠簸
deteriorate	恶化

4.5.2 🔊 听录音

4.5.3 范例

(1) **C:** How many miles do you need to be on present heading?   C：你还需要保持当前航向多少海里？

(2) **C:** How far do you need to keep/track out on present heading?   C：你还需要保持当前航向飞多远？

(3) **C:** You can deviate 10 miles right of track to avoid build-up.   C：可以往航迹右偏10海里避让积雨云。

(4) **C:** When clear of weather, proceed direct to BSE, resume own navigation.   C：无影响后，直飞百色，恢复自主领航。

(5) **C:** Follow the track of the preceding aircraft to avoid build-up.   C：跟着前机航迹避让积雨云。

(6) **C: Report flight conditions.**   C：报告飞行条件。

4.6 航空器加入、穿越或离开航路

当航空器要加入、穿越或离开航路时，必须向管制员提出申请，只有得到管制员的许可之后才可以执行。在相关的通话术语中，"加入""穿越"及"离开"是关键词汇。

4.6.1 单词与词组

join	加入
cross	穿越

leave	离开
rejoin	重新加入
on track	在航迹上

4.6.2 🔊 听录音

1. 加入航路

2. 穿越航路

3. 离开航路

4.6.3 范例

(1) C: CCA1730, **join** A1 at DAL at 5,400 meters.

C：CCA1730，在 DAL 加入 A1，高度 5 400 米。

(2) C: CES5166, **cleared to leave** A1 via DAL VOR.

C：CES5166，可以经由 DAL VOR 离开 A1。

(3) C: ACA026, **cleared to cross** A1 at DAL VOR at 4,500 meters.

C：ACA026，可以在 DAL VOR 穿越 A1，高度 4 500 米。

第 5 章 进近管制——进场阶段

在进近管制进场阶段，航空器的高度、速度和航向变化频度较高，因此关于高度、速度和航向的管制指令使用较多，且通话频率较快。此外，对应不同的进场和进近方式，可使用相应的术语进行表述。

通过本章的学习，应达到以下学习目标：

❖ 掌握进场雷达引导的相关用语；
❖ 掌握航空器高度调整的相关用语；
❖ 掌握航空器速度调整的相关用语；
❖ 掌握航空器进场及进近的相关用语；
❖ 了解 VFR 进场的相关用语；
❖ 了解雷达进近的相关用语。

5.1 进场及进近

当航空器从区域移交至进近管制单位后，管制员需要根据交通情况，为航空器安排着陆次序，及时调整航空器的高度、速度和航向，若有延误，应及时发布延误指令。

5.1.1 单词与词组

ILS	仪表着陆系统
reduce speed to	减速到
resume normal speed	恢复正常速度
maintain present speed	保持现在速度
reduce to minimum approach speed	减到最小进近速度
reduce to minimum clean speed	减到最小光洁速度
no (ATC) speed restrictions	无（ATC）速度限制
vectoring for ILS approach	雷达引导 ILS 进近
vectoring for (position in the circuit)	雷达引导到（起落航线位置）
delay	延误
no delay expected	预计没有延误
holding pattern	等待航线
delay not determined	延误没有确定
straight-in approach	直线进近
terminated	终止
extend downwind	延长三边

cleared for ILS approach	可以 ILS 进近
report established	建立报告
Final	五边（进近管制单位的一个席位）

5.1.2 🔊 听录音

5.1.3 范例

(1) C: AFR102, **report speed**.
P: Speed 250 knots, AFR102.
C: AFR102, **reduce to minimum clean speed**.
P: Reducing to 210 knots, AFR102.

C：AFR102，报告速度。
P：速度 250，AFR102。
C：AFR102，减到最小光洁速度。
P：减速到 210，AFR102。

(2) C: HDA786, **maintain** 250 knots **or greater**, No.1 to land.
P: 250 knots, HDA786.
  (A moment later)
C: HDA786, **resume normal speed**.
P: Normal speed, HDA786.

C：HDA786，速度不小于 250，第一个落地。
P：250，HDA786。
  （稍后）
C：HDA786，恢复正常速度。
P：正常速度，HDA786。

(3) C: AFL3820, **do not exceed** 190 knots, preceding traffic is B777, heavy, **caution wake turbulence**.
P: Not exceed 190 knots, AFL3820.

C：AFL3820，速度不得超过 190，前机 B777，重型，注意尾流。
P：速度不超过 190，AFL3820。

(4) C: KLM4453, Beijing Approach, **maintain present speed**.
P: Maintain present speed, KLM4453.

C：KLM4453，北京进近，保持现在速度。
P：保持现在速度，KLM4453。

(5) C: CSN6136, **no speed restriction**, contact Final 118.2, good day.
P: Roger, 118.2, good day, CSN6136.

C：CSN6136，无速度限制，联系五边 118.2，再见。
P：收到，118.2，再见，CSN6136。

(6) C: CES5166, **reduce to minimum approach speed**.
P: Reducing to minimum approach speed, CES5166.

C：CES5166，减到最小进近速度。
P：减到最小进近速度，CES5166。

(7) C: CSN3102, **confirm RNAV approved**.
P: Affirm RNAV, CSN3102.
C: CSN3102, follow ATAGA1A RNAV

C：CSN3102，证实 RNAV 已批准。
P：是 RNAV，CSN3102。
C：CSN3102，按照 ATAGA1A RNAV

第 5 章　进近管制——进场阶段

Arrival. 进场。

(8) P: Guangzhou Approach, CPA5782, **unable RNAV due equipment**.
C: CPA5782, roger, **report able to resume RNAV**.
P: Wilco, CPA5782.

P：广州进近，CPA5782，由于设备原因不能保持 RNAV。
C：CPA5782，收到，能够恢复 RNAV 时报告。
P：照办，CPA5782。

(9) C: EVA707, turn left heading 090, **report runway in sight**, expect visual approach, Runway 19.
P: Roger, expect visual approach, will report when runway in sight, EVA707.
　　(A moment later)
P: Runway in sight, EVA707.
C: EVA707, follow the A340, **cleared for visual approach**, Runway 19, **caution wake turbulence**. Contact Tower 118.1, good day.
P: Cleared for visual approach, Runway19, contact Tower 118.1, good day.

C：EVA707，左转航向 090，看到跑道报告，预计目视进近，跑道 19。
P：收到，预计目视进近，看到跑道报告，EVA707。
　　(稍后)
P：看到跑道，EVA707。
C：EVA707，跟在 A340 后面，可以目视进近，跑道 19，注意尾流。联系塔台 118.1，再见。
P：可以目视进近，跑道 19，联系塔台 118.1，再见。

(10) C: HVN506, preceding traffic B777 at 9 o'clock, 12 kilometers, report traffic in sight.
P: Traffic in sight, HVN506.
C: HVN506, succeeding traffic 13 kilometers behind you, it'll cross your level by visual separation.
P: Roger, HVN506.

C：HVN506，前机是 B777，在 9 点方位，12 公里，看到活动报告。
P：看到活动，HVN506。
C：HVN506，后机距离你 13 公里，它将使用目视间隔穿越你的高度层。
P：收到，HVN506。

(11) C: CHH7702, **turn left heading 330 immediately to avoid traffic deviating from adjacent approach**, climb to 1,200 meters.

C：CHH7702，立即左转航向 330，避让偏离邻近进近航迹的飞行活动，上升到 1 200 米。

(12) C: ANA5701, I will **take you through the localizer** for separation.

C：ANA5701，因为间隔将引导你穿过航向道。

(13) C：CXA1883, **you have crossed the localizer**, turn left immediately and return to the localizer.

C：CXA1883，你已穿过航向道，立即左转返回航向道。

(14) C: UAL7429, **maintain** 170 **knots** until

C：UAL7429，保持 170 到接地点 7

7 miles from touchdown, contact Tower 118.1, good day.

海里，联系塔台 118.1，再见。

(15) **P:** Dongfang Arrival, CES5121, heavy, maintaining 5,100 meters, approaching VYK, Information C received.
C: CES5121, Dongfang Arrival, radar contact, Information C is valid, **vectoring for ILS approach**, Runway 36R, QNH 1,007.
P: Roger, ILS approach, Runway 36R, QNH 1,007, CES5121.
C: CES5121, turn left heading 350.
P: Left heading 350, CES5121.
C: CES5121, **report speed**.
P: Speed 250 knots, CES5121.
C: CES5121, **reduce to minimum clean speed**.
P: Reducing to 210 knots, CES5121.
C: CES5121, descend to 2,100 meters on QNH 1,006.
P: Descending to 2,100 meters on QNH 1,006, CES5121.
C: CES5121, turn right heading 090 for base.
P: Right heading 090, CES5121.
C: CES5121, **reduce to minimum approach speed**, turn left heading 030, **cleared for ILS approach**, Runway 36R, **report established**.
P: Reducing to minimum approach speed, left heading 030, cleared for ILS approach, Runway 36R, CES5121.
(A moment later)
P: CES5121, established.
C: CES5121, **no ATC speed restrictions**, position 15 kilometers from touchdown, **radar service terminated**, contact tower 118.8, good day.
P: 118.8, good day, CES5121.

P：东方进场，CES5121，重型，5 100 米保持，接近大王庄，通播 C 收到。
C：CES5121，东方进场，雷达看到了，通播 C 有效，雷达引导，ILS 进近，跑道 36 右，修正海压 1 007。
P：收到，ILS 进近，跑道 36 右，修正海压 1 007，CES5121。
C：CES5121，左转航向 350。
P：左转航向 350，CES5121。
C：CES5121，报告速度。
P：速度 250，CES5121。
C：CES5121，减到最小光洁速度。
P：减速到 210，CES5121。
C：CES5121，下降到修正海压 2 100 米，修正海压 1 006。
P：下降到修正海压 2 100 米保持，修正海压 1 006，CES5121。
C：CES5121，右转航向 090 飞向四边。
P：右转航向 090，CES5121。
C：CES5121，减到最小进近速度，左转航向 030，可以 ILS 进近，跑道 36 右，建立报告。
P：减到最小进近速度，左转航向 030，可以 ILS 进近，跑道 36 右，CES5121。
（稍后）
P：CES5121，建立了。
C：CES5121，无 ATC 速度限制，距接地点 15 公里，雷达服务终止，联系塔台 118.8，再见。
P：118.8，再见，CES5121。

(16) **P:** Tianjin Approach, B3213.
C: B3213, Tianjin Approach.
P: B3213, Robinson R44, VFR from Tanggu helicopter airport to Binhai

P：天津进近，B3213。
C：B3213，天津进近。
P：B3213，Robinson R44，目视飞行规则，从塘沽直升机机场飞往滨海国

airport. 600 meters, estimating Binhai airport at 30, Information B.
C: B3213, cleared to Binhai airport, VFR, QNH 1,011.
P: Cleared to Binhai airport, VFR, QNH 1,011, B3213.
C: B3213, report aerodrome in sight.
P: Wilco, B3213.
(A moment later)
P: B3213, aerodrome in sight.
C: B3213, contact Tower 118.1.
P: 118.1, B3213.

际机场。高度 600 米，预计到达滨海机场 30 分，通播 B 收到。
C：B3213，可以目视飞行到滨海国际机场，修正海压 1 011。
P：可以目视飞行到滨海机场，修正海压 1 011，B3213。
C：B3213，能见机场报告。
P：照办，N321EH。
（稍后）
P：B3213，能见机场。
C：B3213，联系塔台 118.1。
P：118.1，B3213。

(17) **P:** Dongfang Approach, CSN3356, request straight-in VOR approach Runway 04.
C: CSN3356, Dongfang Approach, cleared straight-in VOR approach Runway 04.

P：东方进近，CSN3356，请求直线 VOR 进近跑道 04。
C：CSN3356，东方进近，可以直线 VOR 进近跑道 04。

5.2 雷达进近

雷达进近主要有监视雷达进近和精密雷达进近两类，监视雷达进近通常作为一种应急程序。

监视雷达进近（surveillance radar approach，SRA）时，管制员为驾驶员提供航空器距离接地端的距离和建议高度，以便驾驶员能够在指定的跑道上实施进近。

精密雷达进近时，管制员不仅要为航空器提供航向信息，还需要提供高度信息。

5.2.1 单词与词组

surveillance radar approach (SRA)	监视雷达进近
touchdown	接地
obstacle clearance altitude	超障高度
commence	开始
decision altitude	决断高度
decision height	决断高
minimum descent altitude	最低下降高度

5.2.2 🔊 听录音

1. 监视雷达进近

2. 精密雷达进近

5.2.3 范例

(1) C: CSN3106, Dongfang Precision, approaching glide path, **heading is good**.

C：CSN3106，东方精密，正在接近下滑道，航向好。

(2) C: CCA1356, **do not acknowledge further transmissions**, on track, approaching glide path.

C：CCA1356，不要认收下列通话，在航向道上，正在接近下滑道。

(3) C: CAL512, **check your minima**.

C：CAL512，检查最低标准。

(4) C: CHB6263, check wheels down and locked.

C：CHB6263，检查起落架放下锁好。

(5) C: CUA5998, 5 1/2 miles from touchdown, altitude should be 2,000 feet.

C：CUA5998，距离接地 5.5 海里，高度应为 2 000 英尺。

第6章 机场管制——最后进近及着陆阶段

最后进近及着陆阶段包括航空器在五边建立稳定进近、着陆及滑入等常规运行阶段，还包括复飞程序及本场训练。最后进近和着陆阶段是航空器运行最为关键的阶段之一，此时驾驶员的操作、观察等工作负荷大增，因此，管制员标准、正确、适时的通话对保障航空器安全至关重要。此阶段的通话术语相对简练，涉及高度、速度及航向参数的指令不多，而是以"许可"为主。"许可"的结构相对简单，但发送时机非常重要。

通过本章的学习，应达到以下学习目标：

- ❖ 掌握起落航线飞行相关单词和用语；
- ❖ 掌握最后进近与着陆通话用语；
- ❖ 掌握复飞用语；
- ❖ 掌握脱离跑道、滑行入位等指令的格式和用语；
- ❖ 了解本场训练科目；
- ❖ 了解本场训练管制用语。

6.1 起落航线飞行

起落航线分为左起落航线和右起落航线。起飞后向左转弯建立航线叫左起落航线，向右转弯建立航线叫右起落航线，标准起落航线为左起落航线。起落航线通常由五条边、四个转弯（分别称为"一转弯""二转弯""三转弯"和"四转弯"）组成。如下图所示，假设航空器从跑道起飞，做一个左起落航线，航空器离地沿着跑道中心线延长线飞行，这个边叫"一边"（upwind），接着转向"二边"（crosswind），再做一个转弯转向"三边"（downwind），接下来转向"四边"（base），最后通过四转弯转向"五边"（final）准备着陆。

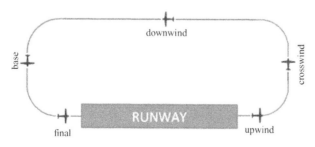

6.1.1 单词与词组

upwind   一边，顶风

turning crosswind	一转弯
crosswind	二边，侧风
turning downwind	二转弯
downwind	三边，顺风
turning base	三转弯
base	四边
turning final	四转弯
final	五边
join	加入
straight-in approach	直线进近
extend downwind	延长三边
orbit	盘旋
make one orbit right	右盘旋一圈
make short approach	做小航线

6.1.2 🔊听录音

6.1.3 范例

(1) P: Dongfang Tower, CCA1726, A320, 10 kilometers north, 900 meters, request joining instructions to land.

C: CCA1726, **join downwind**, Runway 24, wind 270 degrees, 7 m/s, QNH 1,012.

P: Join downwind, Runway 24, QNH 1,012, CCA1726.

P：东方塔台，CCA1726，A320，机场以北 10 公里，900 米保持，请求加入起落航线落地。

C：CCA1726，加入三边，跑道 24，地面风 270 度，7 米每秒，修正海压 1 012。

P：加入三边，跑道 24，修正海压 1 012，CCA1726。

(2) P: Dongfang Tower, BAW1168, A320, 10 kilometers north, 900 meters, request joining instructions to land.

C: BAW1168, **make straight-in approach**, Runway 16, wind 190 degrees, 7 m/s, QNH 1,001.

P: Straight-in approach, Runway 16, QNH 1,001, BAW1168.

P：东方塔台，BAW1168，A320，机场以北 10 公里，900 米保持，请求加入起落航线落地。

C：BAW1168，直线进近，跑道 16，地面风 190 度，7 米每秒，修正海压 1 001。

P：直线进近，跑道 16，修正海压 1 001，BAW1168。

第 6 章 机场管制——最后进近及着陆阶段

(3) P: Dongfang Tower, AMU866, downwind[①].
C: AMU866, No. 2, follow B747 on base.
P: No.2, traffic in sight, AMU866.
P: Dongfang Tower, AMU866, base.
C: AMU866, **Report final**.
P: Wilco, AMU866.
   (A moment later)
P: Dongfang Tower, AMU866, final.
C: AMU866, **continue approach**, wind 270 degrees, 7 m/s.

(4) C: CAL545, **extend downwind**, No. 2, follow A330 on 4 miles final.
P: No. 2, A330 in sight, CAL545.
C: CAL545, **make one orbit right** due traffic on the runway, report again on final.
P: Orbit right, CAL545.
   (A moment later)
C: CAL545, No.1, **make short approach**.
P: Short approach, CAL545.

P：东方塔台，AMU866，三边。
C：AMU866，跟在四边上的B747后面，第二个落地。
P：第二个，看到B747了，AMU866。
P：东方塔台，AMU866，四边。
C：AMU866，五边报。
P：照办，AMU866。
（稍后）
P：东方塔台，AMU866，五边。
C：AMU866，继续进近，地面风270度，7米每秒。

C：CAL545，延长三边，跟在五边4海里A330后面，第二个落地。
P：第二个，看到A330了，CAL545。
C：CAL545，由于跑道上有活动，右盘旋一圈，五边报。
P：右盘旋一圈，CAL545。
（稍后）
C：CAL545，做小航线，第一个落地。
P：做小航线，CAL545。

6.2 最后进近与着陆

最后进近中，当航空器转至五边时，距离接地地带在7公里（或4海里）之内，则报告"五边（final）"；距离接地地带大于7公里（或4海里），则报告"长五边（long final）"。如果航空器做直线进近，距离接地地带15公里（或8海里）时，航空器报告"长五边（long final）"。如果此时未收到着陆许可，则在距离接地地带7公里（或4海里）时，报告"五边（final）"。当航空器处于进近和着陆最后阶段时，除非出现紧急情况，不应向航空器发送指令或信息。

塔台管制员发出着陆许可后，如果条件变化，管制员必须立即通知航空器复飞，同时简要说明复飞原因。着陆或者复飞由驾驶员最后决定，并且对其决定负责。航空器复飞后，塔台管制员应为驾驶员提供复飞程序或航向高度，并将复飞航空器移交给进近管制员。

6.2.1 单词与词组

outer marker　　　　　　　　　　　　　外指点标

---

① 已经加入起落航线的航空器，按照本场运行程序要求，驾驶员需要做常规的位置报告。

go around	复飞
missed approach	复飞（程序）
overshoot	飞越跑道
negative contact	没有看到
advise	告知，建议
minima	最低标准
wind shear	风切变

6.2.2 听录音

6.2.3 范例

(1) **P:** Dongfang Tower, UPS2921, long final.

　　C: UPS2921, Dongfang Tower, **continue approach**, wind 260 degrees, 7 m/s.

　　P: Continue approach, UPS2921.
　　（A moment later）

　　P: Dongfang Tower, UPS2921, final.

　　C: UPS2921, **wind 270 degrees, 7 m/s, Runway 27, cleared to land**.

　　P: Runway 27, cleared to land, UPS2921.

　　P：东方塔台，UPS2921，长五边。

　　C：UPS2921，东方塔台，继续进近，地面风260度，7米每秒。

　　P：继续进近，UPS2921。
　　（稍后）

　　P：东方塔台，UPS2921，五边。

　　C：UPS2921，地面风270度，7米每秒，跑道27，可以落地。

　　P：跑道27，可以落地，UPS2921。

(2) **C:** AAL128, Dongfang Tower, **go around**, aircraft on the runway.

　　P: Dongfang Tower, AAL128, going around.

　　C：AAL128，东方塔台，复飞，跑道上有飞机。

　　P：东方塔台，AAL128，复飞。

(3) **P:** Dongfang Tower, ACA088, **no contact at minima, going around**.

　　C: ACA088, roger, report downwind.

　　P：东方塔台，ACA088，最低高度没有能见地面，复飞。

　　C：ACA088，收到，三边报。

(4) **C:** CPA347, the broken airplane will be towed out of the runway in time, **continue approach, prepare for possible go-around**.

　　C：CPA347，损坏的飞机将被及时拖出跑道，继续进近，做好可能复飞的准备。

6.3 滑入

　　当航空器处于着陆滑跑时，除非完全必要，管制员不应在其结束滑跑前发布滑行指令。一般情况下，航空器在脱离跑道前，应保持在塔台频率上。

6.3.1 单词与词组

fast turnoff	快速脱离道
exit	跑道快速出口
convenient	方便的
available	可用的
vacate	脱离

6.3.2 🔊 听录音

6.3.3 范例

(1) **C1:** HDA841, **vacate runway via Taxiway E**.
P: Vacate runway via Taxiway E, HDA841.
(A moment later)
P: Dongfang Tower, HDA841, runway vacated.
C1: HDA841, contact Dongfang Ground on 121.7, good day.
P: 121.7, HDA841, good day.
P: Dongfang Ground, HDA841, runway vacated.
C2: HDA841, Dongfang Ground, **report follow-me car in sight**.
P: Follow-me car in sight, HDA841.
C2: HDA841, follow the follow-me car, goodbye.
P: Follow the follow-me car, goodbye. HDA841.

C1：HDA841，沿 E 滑行道脱离跑道。
P：E 滑行道脱离跑道，HDA841。
（稍后）
P：东方塔台，HDA841，已脱离跑道。
C1：HDA841，联系东方地面 121.7，再见。
P：121.7，HDA841，再见。
P：东方地面，HDA841，已脱离跑道。
C2：HDA841，东方地面，见引导车报告。
P：看到引导车了，HDA841。
C2：HDA841，跟着引导车滑行，再见。
P：跟着引导车滑行，HDA841，再见。

(2) **C1:** AAL8901, **expedite vacating** runway, aircraft on short final. **When vacated, contact** Dongfang Ground on 119.2, goodbye.
P: Expedite vacating, Dongfang Ground 119.2, AAL8901, goodbye.
(A moment later)
P: Dongfang Ground, AAL8901, runway vacated.
C2: AAL8901, Dongfang Ground, **hold position**, give way to B747 entering Taxiway H.
P: Holding, AAL8901.

C1：AAL8901，加速脱离跑道，短五边有落地飞机。脱离后，联系东方地面 119.2，再见。
P：加速脱离，东方地面 119.2，AAL8901，再见。
（稍后）
P：东方地面，AAL8901，已脱离跑道。
C2：AAL8901，东方地面，原地等待，给正在滑入 H 滑行道的 B747 让路。
P：等待，AAL8901。

	(A moment later)	（稍后）
	C2: AAL8901, taxi to Stand B213 via Taxiway H, D2 and D3, good day.	**C2:** AAL8901，沿滑行道 H、D2 和 D3 滑到停机位 B213，再见。
	P: Stand B213 via Taxiway H, D2 and D3, AAL8901, good day.	**P:** 沿 H、D2 和 D3 滑到停机位 B213，AAL8901，再见。
(3)	**C:** ANA8489, **take first right, report runway vacated**[①].	**C:** ANA8489，前面第一个道口右转，脱离报。
	P: First right, report runway vacated, ANA8489.	**P:** 第一个道口右转，脱离报，ANA8489。
	(A moment later)	（稍后）
	P: Dongfang Tower, ANA8489, runway vacated.	**P:** 东方塔台，ANA8489，脱离跑道。
	C: ANA8489, taxi to Gate 12 via Taxiway C, C3 and C4. **Caution, construction work in progress** adjacent to Gate 12.	**C:** ANA8489，沿滑行道 C、C3 和 C4 滑到停机位 12。注意，停机位 12 旁正在施工。
	P: Gate 12 via Taxiway C, C3 and C4, ANA8489.	**P:** 沿滑行道 C、C3 和 C4 滑到停机位 12，ANA8489。

6.4 本场训练

常见的本场训练的形式包括低空通场、低高度进近和连续起飞等形式。

当驾驶员需要地面帮助目视检查航空器状态时，如起落架是否收放好，起落架舱门是否关闭等，可申请低空通场以低高度飞越塔台或其他观测点，请管制员或机务人员检查。

为了做进近训练，驾驶员可能申请沿跑道或平行于跑道实施进近，但不着陆，这种训练叫作低高度进近。

当驾驶员进行起落航线训练时，为节省滑行时间，可能申请进行连续起飞，即着陆之后继续进行起飞滑跑并起飞。

6.4.1 单词与词组

low approach	低高度进近
touch and go	连续起飞
full stop	全停
congestion	交通拥堵
low pass	低空通场
landing gear	起落架
undercarriage	起落架

---

① 通常在低能见度下使用。

6.4.2 🔊 听录音

1. 低空通场

2. 低高度进近

3. 连续起飞

6.4.3 范例

(1) **P:** Dongfang Tower, AHK8783, our nose gear is jammed, request low pass to have the undercarriage checked.
C: AHK8783, Dongfang Tower, **cleared low pass**, Runway 18, **not below 150 meters**, report final.
P: Runway 18, not below 150 meters, report final, AHK8783.

P：东方塔台，AHK8783，由于前起落架卡住了，请求低空通场进行目视检查。
C：AHK8783，东方塔台，可以低空通场，跑道 18，不低于 150 米，五边报。
P：跑道 18，不低于 150 米，五边报，AHK8783。

(2) **C:** JOY1517, **landing gear appears down**.

C：JOY1517，起落架看起来放下了。

(3) **P:** Dongfang Tower, YZR7991, request low **approach**, Runway 23 for training.
C: YZR7991, Dongfang Tower, **cleared low** approach, Runway 23, not below 150 meters, report final.
P: Runway 23, not below 150 meters, report final, YZR7991.

P：东方塔台，YZR7991，请求低高度进近训练，跑道 23。
C：YZR7991，东方塔台，可以低高度进近，跑道 23，不低于 150 米，五边报。
P：跑道 23，不低于 150 米，五边报，YZR7991。

(4) **P:** Dongfang Tower, N231CL, **request touch and go**.
C: N231CL, Dongfang Tower, cleared touch and go.
P: Cleared touch and go, N231CL.

P：东方塔台，N231CL，请求连续起飞。
C：N231CL，东方塔台，可以连续起飞。
P：可以连续起飞，N231CL。

(5) **P:** Dongfang Tower, CSN6624, request touch and go.
C: CSN6624, Dongfang Tower, unable to approve due traffic congestion, **make full stop**, cleared to land.
P: Cleared to land, full stop, CSN6624.

P：东方塔台，CSN6624，请求连续起飞。
C：CSN6624，东方塔台，由于飞机较多，不能连续起飞，做全停，可以落地。
P：可以落地，做全停，CSN6624。

第7章 紧急情况

紧急情况下的通话与常规通话不同，往往没有明确规定的术语，更多以"明语"进行表达。通常以国际上比较习惯、通用的表达作为参考。通话时，管制员应使用镇定、清楚、明确、自信的语音，放慢语速，避免不必要的重复。

通过本章的学习，应达到以下学习目标：

- ❖ 掌握遇险及紧急情况的发布与认收用语；
- ❖ 掌握遇险及紧急情况的处置与取消用语；
- ❖ 了解特殊情况的类别。

常见紧急情况如表7-1所示。

表7-1

英　文	中　文
bomb threat	炸弹威胁
control system failure	操纵系统故障
power system failure	动力系统故障
total electrical failure	电力系统故障
engine failure	发动机故障
de-icing/anti-icing system failure	除冰/防冰系统故障
windshield（英式英语中为 windscreen）problems	风挡问题
fire in the hold/toilet/cabin	货舱起火/厕所起火/客舱起火
hijack	劫机
radar failure	雷达失效
under carriage failure	起落架故障
fuel problems	燃油问题
communication failure	通信失效
hydraulic system failure	液压系统故障
passenger with a heart attack/ injuries among passengers and cabin crew after severe turbulence/pregnant woman	患心脏病的乘客/严重颠簸导致乘客和空乘人员受伤/孕妇
instrument failure	仪表故障
pressurization system failure/decompression (depressurization)	增压系统故障/失压
bird strike	鸟击
low visibility	低能见度
wind shear	风切变
thunderstorm/icing/turbulence	雷暴/积冰/颠簸

7.1 发布与认收

根据航空器出现问题的严重程度,紧急情况可以分为遇险和紧急。

遇险(distress)是指航空器或航空器上人员遇到迫在眉睫的危险的严重威胁,需要立即得到救助的状态。如果航空器处于遇险状态,驾驶员在给管制员报告时,通常会以"MAYDAY"来开始通话,遇险信号应重复三次,即"MAYDAY, MAYDAY, MAYDAY"。遇险信号比所有通话都具有优先权。

紧急(urgency)是指航空器或航空器上人员的安全受到威胁,但不需要立即援助的一种状态。如果航空器处于紧急状态,驾驶员在给管制员报告时,通常会以"PANPAN"来开始通话,紧急信号应重复三次,即"PANPAN, PANPAN, PANPAN"。除遇险信号以外,紧急信号比其他所有通话都具有优先权。

航空器运行过程中,如果出现了遇险情况,驾驶员一般会按照表 7-2 所示的格式向管制员发布信息。

表 7-2

英 文 格 式	中 文 格 式
① MAYDAY, MAYDAY, MAYDAY	① MAYDAY, MAYDAY, MAYDAY
② ATC unit	② 接收电台的名称
③ aircraft identification	③ 航空器识别标志
④ nature of the distress	④ 遇险的性质
⑤ intention of the person in command and request	⑤ 驾驶员意图和请求
⑥ position, level and heading of the aircraft	⑥ 航空器位置、高度和航向
⑦ any other useful information	⑦ 其他有用信息

航空器运行过程中,如果出现了紧急情况,驾驶员一般会按照表 7-3 所示的格式向管制员发布信息。

表 7-3

英 文 格 式	中 文 格 式
① PANPAN, PANPAN, PANPAN	① PANPAN, PANPAN, PANPAN
② ATC unit	② 接收电台的名称
③ aircraft identification	③ 航空器识别标志
④ nature of the urgency	④ 紧急的性质
⑤ intention of the person in command and request	⑤ 驾驶员意图和请求
⑥ position, level and heading of the aircraft	⑥ 航空器位置、高度和航向
⑦ any other useful information	⑦ 其他有用信息

7.1.1 单词与词组

MAYDAY　　　　　　　　　　　　　遇险的话呼
PANPAN　　　　　　　　　　　　　紧急的话呼
port　　　　　　　　　　　　　　　左(舷/翼)

starboard	右（舷/翼）
ditch	水上迫降
extinguish	扑灭
dump fuel	放油
burn off	消耗
roger MAYDAY	收到 MAYDAY
intoxicated	醉酒
radioactive	放射性的

7.1.2 🔊听录音

7.1.3 范例

(1) **C:** CKK206, Dongfang Approach, **roger MAYDAY/PANPAN**.

C: CKK206，东方进近，收到 MAYDAY/PANPAN。

(2) **P:** CSH9070, position POU, emergency descent to 3,600 meters due to decompression.
C: Attention, all aircraft in the vicinity of POU, **emergency descent in progress** from 8,900 meters to 3,600 meters.

P：CSH9070，位置平洲，由于失压，紧急下降到 3 600 米。
C：在平洲附近的所有航空器请注意，有航空器正在紧急下降，高度 8 900 米到 3 600 米。

(3) **P:** G-BDES, **transmitting blind due to receiver failure**. G-BDES 7,500 meters, heading 110, over CHG VOR this time, descending to be at 3,600 meters over GOL, standard arrival procedure, next for landing Runway 36 at Dongfang.

P：G-BDES，接收机失效，盲发。G-BDES，高度 7 500 米，航向 110，CHG 上方，下降到 3 600 米通过 GOL，标准进场程序，东方机场跑道 36 落地。

(4) **C:** All aircraft, Dongfang Control, **fuel dumping in progress**, on radial 230 JUI VOR, ranging from 15 to 20 miles, avoid flight below 600 meters within 10 miles of the fuel dumping track.

C：全体注意，东方区域，有航空器正在放油中，JUI 230 度径向线，范围 15 到 20 海里，避免进入放油航迹下方 600 米，水平 10 海里范围内。

7.2 处置与取消

遇险（或紧急）呼叫通常应在当前使用的频率上完成。如果波道内通话繁忙，管制员认为将遇险航空器移交到另一频率将有利于问题的解决，可以实施通话强制静默；如果将其他航空器移交到另一频率，而专心在当前频率协助遇险航空器更有效，则可指挥其他航空器联系另一频率。当管制员得知遇险结束，应通知所有相关电台。

7.2.1 单词和词组

stop transmitting	停止通信
cancel distress	取消遇险
distress traffic ended	遇险活动结束
rear	后部，尾部
smoke	烟
cargo hold	货舱
fire truck	消防车
dangerous goods	危险品
persons on board	机上人数

7.2.2 🔊听录音

7.2.3 范例

(1) **C: All stations**, Dongfang Approach, **stop transmitting, MAYDAY**.

C：全体注意，东方进近，停止通信，MAYDAY。

(2) **C:** MAYDAY, G-BCDO, Dongfang Approach, contact Control on 127.1.

C：MAYDAY，G-BCDO，东方进近，联系区域127.1。

(3) **P:** Dongfang Approach, G-BCDO, **cancel distress**, engine restarted.
C: MAYDAY, all stations, Dongfang Approach, time 1325, **distress traffic G-BCDO ended**.

P：东方进近，G-BCDO，取消遇险，发动机重启了。
C：MAYDAY 全体注意，东方进近，1325分，G-BCDO 遇险活动结束。

"听录音"原文

第2章 机场管制——起飞前与起飞阶段

2.1 无线电检查

P: Dongfang Ground, CSN3401, radio check on 121.5. How do you read?

C: CSN3401, Dongfang Ground, readability 5.

2.2 离场条件

2.2.1 离场条件

P: Pudong Ground, CXA101, request departure information.

C: CXA101, Pudong Ground, departure Runway 17, wind 180 degrees, 4 m/s, QNH 1,015, temperature 28, dew point 21, RVR 550 meters.

2.2.2 机场通播

Beijing Capital Airport Information D, 0930 UTC, ILS approach, Runway 18R, runway surface wet, braking action good, wind 300 degrees, 5 m/s, CAVOK, temperature 28, dew point 25, QNH 1,010, no significant other information. On initial contact advise you have Information D.

2.3 重要机场情报

C: UPS102, Dongfang Tower, runway surface condition, Runway 36L, centerline lighting unserviceable.

2.4 放行许可

P: Dongfang Delivery, CSH9070, destination Shanghai, with Information C, request ATC clearance.

C: CSH9070, Dongfang Delivery, cleared to Shanghai via flight planned route, ALPHA11D Departure, initial climb to 900 meters on QNH 1,013, request level change for 9,500 meters en route, squawk 2013, after departure, contact Approach 119.1.

P: Cleared to Shanghai via flight planned route, ALPHA11D Departure, initial climb to 900 meters on QNH 1,013, request level change for 9,500 meters en route, squawk 2013, after departure, contact Approach 119.1, CSH9070.

C: CSH9070, read-back correct.

2.5 推出开车

P: Beijing Ground, CSN303, Stand A5, request push-back and start up.
C: CSN303, push-back and start up approved.

2.6 滑出

P: Beijing Ground, CAL501, request taxi.
C: CAL501, Beijing Ground, taxi to holding point K2, Runway 36R via Taxiway K, hold short of Runway 36R.

2.7 起飞

C: CSN2105, Dongfang Tower, line up, Runway 18L.
P: Lining up, Runway 18L, CSN2105.
C: CSN2105, wind 240 degrees, 10 m/s, Runway 18L, cleared for take-off.
P: Cleared for takeoff, Runway 18L, CSN2105.

第3章 进近管制——离场阶段

3.1 雷达管制用语

C: CPA295, confirm squawking 3426.
P: Affirm, CPA295.
C: CPA295, radar contact, maintain 9,800 meters, continue present heading,
P: Roger, maintaining 9,800 meters, continue present heading, CPA295.
C: CPA295, turn left heading 210.
P: Left heading 210, CPA295

3.2 离场指令

C: CCA1352, wind 350 degrees, 5 m/s, Runway 36, cleared for take-off.
P: Runway 36, cleared for take-off, CCA1352.
　　(A moment later)
P: Dongfang Departure, CCA1352, airborne at 18, passing 130 meters climbing to 900 meters.
C: CCA1352, Dongfang Departure, radar contact, follow YV 51 Departure, continue climb to 2,700 meters on QNH 1,011.
P: Climbing to 2,700 meters on QNH 1,011, YV 51D Departure, CCA1352.
C: CCA1352, continue climb to 5,400 meters on standard, climb at 2,000 ft/min or greater.
P: Climbing to 5,400 meters at 2,000 ft/min or greater, CCA1352.
　　(A moment later)
P: CCA1352, maintaining 5,400 meters.
C: CCA1352, roger.
C: CCA1352, contact Dongfang Control on 120.1, good day.
P: 120.1 for Control, CCA1352, good day.

3.3 飞行活动通报

C: CSN3369, Dongfang Control, unknown traffic, 2 o'clock, 10 kilometers, crossing right to left.

P: Looking out, CSN3369. Request vectors.

C: CSN3369, avoiding action. Turn right 30 degrees immediately and report heading.

P: Turning right 30 degrees, heading 090, CSN3369.

C: CSN3369, now clear of traffic. Resume own navigation to XFA.

第4章 区域管制

4.1 高度信息

P: Beijing Control, CCA1331, over HUR, maintaining 4,500 meters.

C: CCA1331, Beijing Control, radar contact, climb to and maintain 6,300 meters.

P: Climbing to 6,300 meters, CCA1331.

C: CCA1331, continue climbing to 8,900 meters, report reaching.

P: Climbing to 8,900 meters, CCA1331.

(A moment later)

P: CCA1331, approaching 8,900 meters.

C: CCA1331, maintain 8,900 meters, contact Dongfang Control on 123.4, good day.

P: Dongfang Control, 123.4, good day.

4.2 位置信息

P: Dongfang Control, CCA4378, ECH at 35, maintaining 10,400 meters, estimating MEDAL at 48.

C: CCA4378, roger, next report at COAST.

4.3 航路等待

C: CCA1331, Dongfang Control, cleared to MKE, maintain 7,500 meters, hold inbound track 180 degrees, left hand pattern, outbound time one and a half minutes, expect further clearance at 17.

P: Roger, hold at MKE, inbound track 180 degrees, outbound time one and a half minutes, left hand pattern, CCA1331.

4.4 RVSM 运行与 SLOP

C: AAR311, Dongfang Control, confirm RVSM approved.

P: Dongfang Control, AAR311, Negative RVSM.

C: AAR311, unable issue clearance into RVSM airspace, maintain 8,400 meters.

P: Maintaining 8,400 meters, AAR311.

4.5 绕飞雷雨

P: Beijing Control, CCA1730, we have an indication of severe weather 30 kilometers ahead. Request to turn right to go round it.

C: CCA1730, Beijing Control. Negative. Due to the restricted area, turn left 30 degrees and track out 35 kilometers, report clear of the build-ups.

P: Turning 30 degrees left and 35 kilometers out, CCA1730.

(A moment later)

P: Beijing Control, CCA1730, we're clear of CBs now.

C: Roger, CCA1730, turn right heading to come back on track.

4.6 航空器加入、穿越或离开航路

1. 加入航路

P: Dongfang Control, B1213.

C: B1213, Dongfang Control.

P: B1213, request clearance to join G17 at ANDIN.

C: B1213, cleared to Nanyuan, flight planned route, 3,600 meters. Join G17 at ANDIN at 3,600 meters.

P: Cleared to Nanyuan via ANDIN, flight planned route, 3,600 meters. To enter controlled airspace 3,600 meters, B1213.

C: B1213, read-back correct.

2. 穿越航路

P: Dongfang Control, B1716.

C: B1716, Dongfang Control.

P: B1716, Yun-7, 20 miles north of KIG VOR, 2,400 meters, KIG VOR at 33, request clearance to cross airway V21 at KIG VOR.

C: B1716, cleared to cross V21 at KIG VOR, 2,400 meters.

P: Cleared to cross V21 at KIG VOR, 2,400 meters, B1716.

C: B1716, report at KIG VOR.

P: Wilco, B1716.

3. 离开航路

C: B2341, Dongfang Control, cleared to leave A1 via JUI VOR. Maintain 4,500 meters while in controlled airspace.

P: Cleared to leave A1 via JUI VOR. Maintaining 4,500 meters while in controlled airspace, B2341.

第 5 章 进近管制——进场阶段

5.1 进场及进近

P: Beijing Arrival, CXA8101, 5,100 meters maintaining, Information W received.

C1: CXA8101, Beijing Arrival, radar contact. Follow JB7A RNAV arrival, expect radar vector for ILS approach, Runway 36L, Information W is valid.

P: ILS approach, Runway 36L, CXA8101.

C1: CXA8101, descend to 3,600 meters on standard.

P: Descending to 3,600 meters on standard, CXA8101.

C1: CXA8101, descend to 1,800 meters on QNH 1,006.

P: Descending to 1,800 meters on QNH 1,006, CXA8101.

C1: CXA8101, contact Beijing Final 126.1, good day.

P: Final 126.1, good day, CXA8101.

   (A moment later)

P: Beijing Final, CXA8101, 1,800 meters maintaining.

C2: CXA8101, Beijing Final, landing Runway 36L.

P: Runway 36L, CXA8101.

C2: CXA8101, reduce speed to 180 knots.

P: Reducing speed to 180 knots, CXA8101.

C2: CXA8101, turn right heading 020, cleared for ILS approach, Runway 36L, report established on localizer.

P: Right heading 020, ILS approach, Runway 36L, will report established, CXA8101.

   (A moment later)

P: CXA8101, established localizer, Runway 36L.

C2: CXA8101, continue approach, Runway 36L, contact Tower 124.3, good day.

P: Continue approach, Runway 36L, 124.3, good day, CXA8101.

5.2　雷达进近

1. 监视雷达进近

C: CCA1501, Dongfang Radar, this will be a surveillance radar approach, Runway 18, terminating at 1/2 mile from touchdown, obstacle clearance altitude 500 feet, maintain 2,000 feet, check your minima.

2. 精密雷达进近

C: CSN3106, Dongfang Precision, approaching glide path, heading is good.

P: Dongfang Precision, CSN3106.

C: CSN3106, do not ackonwlege further transmissions, on track, approaching glide path.

C: CSN3106, check your minima.

C: CSN3106, commence descent now at 500 feet.

C: CSN3106, check wheels down and locked.

第 6 章　机场管制——最后进近及着陆阶段

6.1　起落航线飞行

P: Dongfang Tower, B-7321, Yun-7, 10 kilometers north of the field, 900 meters, request joining instructions to land.

C: B-7321, Dongfang Tower, join downwind, Runway 36, wind 150 degrees, 10 m/s, QNH 1,015.

P: Join downwind, Runway 36, QNH 1,015, B-7321.

6.2 最后进近与着陆
C: CES5412, Dongfang Tower, wind calm, Runway 36L, cleared to land.
P: Runway 36L, cleared to land, CES5412.

6.3 滑入
C1: CCA1320, Dongfang Tower, wind 110 degrees, 5 m/s, Runway 09, cleared to land.
P: Cleared to land, Runway 09, CCA1320.
　(A moment later)
C1: CCA1320, take first left, when vacated, contact Ground 118.35.
P: First left, 118.35, CCA1320.
　(A moment later)
P: Dongfang Ground, CCA1320, runway vacated.
C2: CCA1320, Dongfang Ground, taxi to Stand 28 via Taxiway A and C.
P: Taxi to Stand 28 via Taxiway A and C, CCA1320.

6.4 本场训练
1. 低空通场
P: Dongfang Tower, B2711, request low pass for landing gear check.
C: B2711, Dongfang Tower, cleared low pass, Runway 18R.
2. 低高度进近
P: Dongfang Tower, B3644, request low approach and overshoot for another approach training.
C: B3644, Dongfang tower, cleared low approach, Runway 18L.
3. 连续起飞
P: Dongfang Tower, G-ABCD, request touch and go.
C: G-ABCD, Dongfang Tower, cleared touch and go.
P: Cleared touch and go, G-ABCD.

第7章 紧急情况

7.1 发布与认收
P: MAYDAY MAYDAY MAYDAY, Dongfang Tower, G-BYCM, DC-10, port engine on fire. Position 15 kilometers south of Dongfang, 1,200 meters, losing altitude. Heading 010. Request straight-in approach to Dongfang.

C: G-BYCM, Dongfang Tower, roger MAYDAY.

7.2　处置与取消

P: MAYDAY, MAYDAY, MAYDAY, Dongfang Control, D-BIXT. We have fire in the rear toilet. We're descending to 4,500 meters. Request an emergency landing at Dongfang. Position 50 miles west of Dongfang. Heading 075.

C: D-BIXT, Dongfang Control, roger MAYDAY. Break, break, all stations on 126.3, stop transmitting, MAYDAY.

(A moment later)

P: MAYDAY. D-BIXT. Fire now under control. Cancel distress.

C: Roger, D-BIXT. MAYDAY, all stations, distress traffic ended.

附录A 国内常见航空公司的代码、话呼及公司名称

国内常见航空公司

三字码	二字码	英语话呼	中文话呼	公司名称
AHK	LD	AIR HONG KONG	香港货运	香港华民航空
AMU	NX	AIR MACAU	澳门	澳门航空
CAO	CA	AIR CHINA FREIGHT	凤凰	中国国际货运航空
CBJ	JD	CAPITAL JET	神鹿	北京首都航空
CCA	CA	AIR CHINA	国际	中国国际航空
CDG	SC	SHANDONG	山东	山东航空
CES	MU	CHINA EASTERN	东方	中国东方航空
CHB	PN	WEST CHINA	西部	中国西部航空
CHH	HU	HAINAN	海南	海南航空
CKK	CK	CARGO KING	货航	中国货运航空
CQH	9C	AIR SPRING	春秋	春秋航空
CQN	OQ	CHONG QING	重庆	重庆航空
CPA	CX	CATHAY	国泰	国泰航空
CSC	3U	SI CHUAN	四川	四川航空
CSH	FM	SHANGHAI AIR	上航	上海航空
CSN	CZ	CHINA SOUTHERN	南方	中国南方航空
CSS	O3	SHUN FENG	顺丰	顺丰航空
CSZ	ZH	SHENZHEN AIR	深圳	深圳航空
CUA	KN	LIANHANG	联航	中国联合航空
CXA	MF	XIAMEN AIR	白鹭	厦门航空
CYZ	8Y	CHINA POST	邮政	中国邮政航空
DER	DA	DEER JET	金鹿	金鹿航空
DKH	HO	AIR JUNEYAO	吉祥	吉祥航空
EPA	DZ	DONGHAI AIR	东海	深圳东海航空
GCR	GS	BOHAI	渤海	天津航空
GDC	CN	GRAND CHINA	大新华	大新华航空
HBH	NS	HEBEI AIR	河北	河北航空
HDA	KA	DRAGON	港龙	国泰港龙航空
HKE	UO	HONGKONG SHUTTLE	香港	香港快运航空
HXA	G5	CHINA EXPRESS	华夏	华夏航空
JAE	JI	JADE CARGO	翡翠	翡翠国际货运航空

附录 A　国内常见航空公司的代码、话呼及公司名称

续表

三字码	二字码	英语话呼	中文话呼	公司名称
JOY	JR	JOY AIR	幸福	幸福航空
KNA	KY	KUNMING AIR	昆航	昆明航空
KPA	VD	KUN PENG	鲲鹏	鲲鹏航空
LKE	8L	LUCKY AIR	祥鹏	祥鹏航空
OKA	BK	OKAY JET	奥凯	奥凯航空
SHQ	F4	SHANGHAI CARGO	上货航	上海国际货运航空
TBA	TV	TIBET	西藏	西藏航空
UEA	EU	UNITED EAGLE	锦绣	成都航空
YZR	Y8	YANGTZE RIVER	扬子江	扬子江快运
CCD	CA	XIANGJIAN	响箭	大连航空
CDC	GJ	HUALONG	华龙	浙江长龙货运航空

附录 B 国外常见航空公司的代码、话呼及公司名称

国外常见航空公司

三字码	二字码	英文话呼	英文名称	中文名称
AAL	AA	AMERICAN	American Airlines	美国航空
AAR	OZ	ASIANA	Asiana Airlines	韩亚航空
ABW	RU	AIRBRIDGE CARGO	Airbridge Cargo Airlines	俄罗斯空桥货运航空
ACA	AC	AIR CANADA	Air Canada	加拿大航空
AEA	UX	EUROPA	Air Europa	西班牙欧洲航空
AFG	FG	ARIANA	Ariana Afghan Airlines	阿里亚那阿富汗航空
AFL	SU	AEROFLOT	Aeroflot - Russian Airlines	俄罗斯航空
AFR	AF	AIR FRANS	Air France	法国航空
AIC	AI	AIR INDIA	Air India Limited	印度航空
ALK	UL	SRILANKAN	Srilankan Airlines	斯里兰卡航空
ANA	NH	ALL NIPPON	All Nippon Airways	全日空航空
ANZ	NZ	NEW ZEALAND	Air New Zealand	新西兰航空
AUA	OS	AUSTRIAN	Austrian Airlines	奥地利航空
AZA	AZ	ALITALIA	Alitalia Societa Aerea Italiana S.P.A	意大利航空
BAW	BA	SPEEDBIRD	British Airways	英国航空
BKP	PG	BANGKOK AIR	Bangkok Airways	泰国曼谷航空
CEB	5J	CEBU AIR	Cebu Pacific Air	菲律宾宿务太平洋航空
CLX	CV	CARGOLUX	Cargolux Airlines International S.A.	卢森堡货运航空
DAL	DL	DELTA	Delta Air Lines	美国达美航空
DLH	LH	LUFTHANSA	Deutsche Lufthansa, AG, Koeln	德国汉莎航空
EIA	EZ	EVERGREEN	Evergreen International Airlines	美国长青航空
ELY	LY	ELAL	EL AL - Israel Airlines	以色列航空
FDX	FX	FEDEX	Federal Express	美国联邦快递
FIN	AY	FINN AIR	Finnair OYJ	芬兰航空
GEC	LH	LUFTHANSA CARGO	Lufthansa Cargo AG, Frankfurt	德国汉莎货运航空
GFA	GF	GULF AIR	Gulf Air	阿联酋海湾航空
GIA	GA	INDONESIA	Garuda Indonesia Airways, PT.	印度尼西亚鹰航空
HVN	VN	VIET NAM AIRLINES	Hang Khong Viet Nam	越南航空
IAW	IW	IRAQI	Iraqi Airways	伊拉克航空
IRA	IR	IRAN AIR	Iran Air	伊朗航空
JAL	JL	JAPAN AIR	Japan Airlines	日本航空

续表

三字码	二字码	英文话呼	英文名称	中文名称
KAC	KU	KUWAITI	Kuwait Airways	科威特航空
KAL	KE	KOREAN AIR	Korean Air Lines	大韩航空
KLM	KL	KLM	KLM Royal Dutch Airlines	荷兰皇家航空
KOR	JS	AIR KORYO	Air Koryo	朝鲜高丽航空
KZR	KC	ASTANALINE	Air Astana	哈斯克斯坦阿斯塔那航空
MAS	MH	MALAYSIAN	Malaysia Airlines	马来西亚航空
MGL	OM	MONGOL AIR	Mongolian Airlines	蒙古航空
MPH	MP	MARTIN AIR	Martinair Holland N.V.	荷兰马丁航空
MSR	MS	EGYPT AIR	Egypt Air	埃及航空
MXA	MX	MEXICANA	Mexicana Airlines	墨西哥航空
NCA	KZ	NIPPON GARGO	Nippon Cargo Airlines	日本货运航空
OAL	OA	OLYMPIC	Olympic Air	奥林匹克航空
OEA	OX	ORIENT THAI	Orient Thai Airlines	泰国东方航空
PAA	PA	CLIPPER	Pan American Airways	美国泛美航空
PAC	PO	POLAR	Polar Air Cargo Worldwide	美国博立航空
PAL	PR	PHILIPPINE	Philippine Air Lines	菲律宾航空
PIA	PK	PAKISTAN	Pakistan International Airlines	巴基斯坦国际航空
QFA	QF	QANTAS	Qantas Airways	澳大利亚快达航空
QTR	QR	QATARI	Qatar Airways	卡塔尔航空
RBA	BI	BRUNEI	Royal Brunei Airlines	文莱皇家航空
RNA	RA	ROYAL NEPAL	Royal Nepal Airlines	尼泊尔皇家航空
SAA	SA	SPRINGBOK	South African Airways	南非航空
SAS	SK	SCANDINAVIAN	Scandinavian Airlines System	北欧航空
SBI	S7	SIBERIAN AIRLINES	Siberia Airlines	俄罗斯西伯利亚航空
SIA	SQ	SINGAPORE	Singapore Airlines	新加坡航空
SLK	MI	SILKAIR	Silkair	新加坡胜安航空
SVA	SV	SAUDIA	Saudi Arabian Airlines	沙特阿拉伯航空
SWR	LX	SWISS	Swiss International Air Lines	瑞士国际航空
TAY	3V	QUALITY	TNT Airways	比利时 TNT 航空
THA	TG	THAI	Thai Airways International	泰国国际航空
THY	TK	TURKISH	Turkish Airlines	土耳其航空
UAE	EK	EMIRATES	Emirates	阿联酋航空
UAL	UA	UNITED	United Airlines	美国联合航空
UKR	6U	AIR UKRAINE	Air Ukraine	乌克兰航空
UPS	5X	UPS	United Parcel Service	美国联合包裹航空
UZB	HY	UZBEK	Uzbekistan Airways	乌兹别克斯坦航空
VIR	VS	VIRGIN	Virgin Atlantic	英国维珍航空

参 考 文 献

[1] International Civil Aviation Organization. Manual of radiotelephony (Doc 9432 AN/925), 2007.
[2] 中国民用航空局. 空中交通无线电通话用语指南[M]. 成都：西南交通大学出版社, 2005.
[3] 杜实. 空中交通监视服务[M]. 北京：中国民航出版社， 2012.
[4] 闫少华. 非常规陆空通话英语[M]. 北京：中国民航出版社，2008.
[5] 刘继新. 特殊情况下的无线电通话用语[M]. 北京：国防工业出版社，2010.
[6] International Civil Aviation Organization. Manual on the implementation of ICAO language proficiency requirements (Doc 9835 AN/453), 2010.
[7] International Civil Aviation Organization. Aeronautical telecommunications (Annex 10), 2006.
[8] International Civil Aviation Organization. Air traffic management (Doc 4444 ATM/501), 2007.
[9] International Civil Aviation Organization. Designators for aircraft operating agencies, aeronautical authorities and services (Doc 8585/171), 2015.